W9-BYN-793

Saddam's Mystery Babylon

Virtually all Scripture references are quoted from the King James translation of the Holy Bible. To clarify some meanings, the German translation of Dr. Martin Luther and the JPS translation of the Hebrew text for the Old Testament are used in this book.

Saddam's Mystery Babylon
Copyright © 1998 by Arno Froese
West Columbia, South Carolina 29170
Published by The Olive Press, a division of Midnight Call Ministries
West Columbia, SC 29170 U.S.A.

Copy typist: Lynn Jeffcoat
Proofreaders: Pattie Lalonde, Angie Peters
Layout/Design: James Rizzuti
Lithography: Simon Froese
Cover Design: J Spurling

Library of Congress Cataloging-in-Publication Data

Froese, Arno—Rizzuti, James—Malgo, Dr. Wim
 Saddam's Mystery Babylon
 ISBN 0-937422-40-1

Second Printing December 1998

Printed in the United States of America

*This book is dedicated to the
Church of Jesus Christ worldwide.*

Contents

A NOTE FROM THE AUTHOR

The book you are reading came about spontaneously. In the early Spring of 1998, I started to review some of my manuscripts for the planned book, *One Shall Be Taken, the Other Left Behind*. That subject primarily deals with the Blessed Hope of the church: the Rapture.

Then, we heard so much about the Middle East, particularly Iraq. The media had a feast-day again, proclaiming in detail all the events that happened hour-by-hour, day-by-day in Iraq, the ancient land of Babylon.

At the end of March 1998, we had planned a tour to the land of Israel. Some of the participants were uneasy, asking questions about Israel's security. The nightly news showed how Israelis were being supplied with gas mask just in case there would be another missile attack.

The possibility of the ruthless leader, Saddam Hussein, using chemical or biological weapons had to be considered.

It was my task to calm down concerned travelers with the simple truth that Israel is one of the safest countries in the world. I also stressed that, contrary to public opinion, the United States is still the most dangerous country in the developed world. I explained statistical facts which clearly showed that to live in America is more dangerous than embarking on a Holy Land tour to Israel.

To this day, I don't know whether my persistence in believing in the security of Israel was decisive to our co-travelers, but not one of the whole group cancelled the tour because of security concerns. When we arrived in Israel, we noticed that tourism was definitely down. Some estimates ranged from 30-50% cancellation of reservations.

During the early preparation for the tour, I concerned myself with Saddam Hussein and ancient Babylon more than ever before. Suddenly, there was quite a volume of material that urgently needed to be released in this book.

As you read it, you will notice that the center of the message revolves around the title: "Saddam's Mystery Babylon." We confirmed that Babylon, based on the Holy Scripture, is the first power structure, the first Gentile world empire. In the last Book of the Bible, we read about another Babylon called "Mystery Babylon." This last identity is the final power structure of the Gentiles and will include the whole world. Thus, between the first Babylon and the last, "Mystery Babylon," we have the history of the Gentiles.

The fact that in recent years, Iraq, the country which was known as Babylon in ancient time, has made the headlines, shows us that God is doing something in the Middle East that we might not have taken much notice of earlier.

In this book, I explain that the spirit of Babylon was present at the beginning with King Nebuchadnezzar and will be shown even more prominently during the last empire ruled by the man called the Antichrist. Second Thessalonians 2:4 describes him with these words, *"Who opposeth and exalteth himself above all that is called God, or that is worshipped; so that he as God sitteth in the Temple of God, shewing himself that he is God."*

The Scripture tells us that all world empires will, in the end, be destroyed by a stone, which we know is the Lord Jesus Christ. Therefore, it should be no surprise to see the reawakening of the ancient empires such as Babylon (Iraq), Persia (Iran), Greece and Rome (Europe). These ancient empires must become recognizable so they can be destroyed. You can't destroy something that doesn't exist!

Only a hundred years ago, the Middle East was asleep. No one really bothered much with it, but since the reappearing of the State of Israel, the Middle East has become the focal point of the world.

It's important to point out that we don't claim to have all knowledge regarding Bible prophecy, nor can we exactly predict future developments. All of our messages are subject to correction, reproof, and revision. We confess with the Apostle Paul, *"For we know in part, and we prophesy in part. But, when that which is perfect is come, then that which is in part shall be done away"* (1st Corinthians 13:9–10). Therefore, we highlight the parts which we know. For example, Israel exists, the four ancient world empires are identifiable today, the world is becoming united politically, economically, and religiously. We would be guilty of not doing our duty would we fail to publish these truths and make them known to the church.

I've asked my associate, James Rizzuti, to write specifically about Iraq and its leader, Saddam Hussein. He's done an excellent job in researching some of the facts needed to understand the background of this man and the country.

Furthermore, I felt it beneficial to include a chapter by Dr. Wim Malgo, the founder of Midnight Call Ministry. The title, "Jerusalem or Babylon," presents a very challenging spiritual application for the believer.

It's my sincere prayer that the pages of this book will contribute to your better understanding of the times in which we live. I'm perfectly convinced that the coming of the Lord is rapidly drawing nearer, and we truly may expect Him at any moment!

—Arno Froese
July, 1998

FOREWORD

The clarity of explaining the difference between ancient Babylon and the yet not clearly identified "Mystery Babylon" is a topic that Arno Froese has dealt with very well.

He takes great pain to support scriptural statements with historical documentation to reveal what entity the Bible is warning us about when it refers to "Mystery Babylon."

This book will lay to rest dozens of speculations regarding Saddam Hussein's rebuilding of ancient Babylon, intending it to be the world capital for the future.

Arno Froese convincingly demonstrates fulfillment of Bible prophecy based on real events, real countries, and real times.

I congratulate him for a job well done and pray that this book will be distributed widely for the edification of the church.

I must add that his international view quite often collides with our America-first ideas which have been molded by tradition, but he leaves little room for argument by using decisive Scriptures solidly backed with recent historical events.

"Mystery Babylon" is real. The Antichrist spirit is at work and success is all but guaranteed as demonstrated by the undeniable victory of globalism. These frightening facts are offset, however, by Arno Froese's clear proclamation that only Jesus will establish true peace and lasting prosperity for Israel and the world.

—Dr. Dave Breese
July, 1998

CHAPTER ONE

Gentile World Rulership

Summary

Based on Bible prophecy, the European "iron empire" must spread around the world and solidify all the nations into a global society. Europe is already the richest and most sophisticated continent on Earth. With these facts in mind, we will analyze other entities for consideration for the title, "Mystery Babylon."

This book, *Saddam's Mystery Babylon*, is the result of many years of study comparing the prophetic Word to world history, present-day events, and the future. Throughout this book, we will concern ourselves repeatedly with God's chosen people, the Jews, and the Gentiles, who make up the rest of the world. We will also identify the church, which is made up of Jews and Gentiles who believe in Jesus. When the Lord Jesus says, *"Salvation is of the Jews,"* that statement is not exclusively limited to a person's individual salvation, but it includes God's entire creation: all that is included in the first verse of the Bible, *"In the beginning God created the heaven and the earth."*

Scripture clearly indicates that through the Jews, peace will be established on Earth. In contrast, we will see how the Gentiles attempt to produce world peace. The Bible teaches that peace will be brought forth by the Prince of Peace, the Messiah of Israel, the Savior of the world.

Therefore, it is necessary for the Gentiles to produce a counterfeit figurehead capable of uniting the diverse people of the world under his rulership, which will lead to temporary peace on Earth.

It is important to emphasize here in the beginning that no matter how successful the new world systems of the Gentiles will be, ultimately, their attempt to create lasting peace and prosperity will end in the greatest catastrophe the world has ever known: the Great Tribulation.

The prosperity after which the world is so frantically chasing can only be achieved through peace. Countries at war lack prosperity. War destroys; peace builds. However, real peace can never be established without salvation in Jesus Christ. At this point, real peace is only attainable for the *individual* who trusts in the already accomplished work of the Lord Jesus Christ. They are the only ones who know what the Bible means when it describes, *"...peace that passeth all understanding.*" Nevertheless, peace is not perpetually limited to the individual, because the God of Israel, the Creator of heaven and Earth, has promised to give real peace to Israel and then to the world. But we must reiterate that real peace, the kind that produces lasting prosperity, can only be attained by salvation.

Jews and Gentiles

The Bible clearly distinguishes between the Jews and Gentiles. The Gentiles are grouped into four successive historical divisions: the Babylonian kingdom under Nebuchadnezzar; the Medo-Persian kingdom; the Greek kingdom; and the Roman world empire. All nations, no matter how great or small, fall into one of these categories over the course of history.

The Four-fold Gentile Empires

The four Gentile world empires are described for us in Daniel chapter 7, *"Daniel spake and said, I saw in my vision by night, and, behold, the four winds of the heaven strove upon the great sea.*

"And four great beasts came up from the sea, diverse one from another.

"The first was like a lion, and had eagle's wings: I beheld till the wings thereof were plucked, and it was lifted up from the earth, and made stand upon the feet as a man, and a man's heart was given to it.

"And behold another beast, a second, like to a bear, and it raised up itself on one side, and it had three ribs in the mouth of it between the teeth of it: and they said thus unto it, Arise, devour much flesh.

"After this I beheld, and lo another, like a leopard, which had upon the back of it four wings of a fowl; the beast had also four heads; and dominion was given to it.

"After this I saw in the night visions, and behold a fourth beast, dreadful and terrible, and strong exceedingly; and it had great iron teeth: it devoured and brake in pieces, and stamped the residue with the feet of it: and it was diverse from all the beasts that were before it; and it had ten horns" (Daniel 7:2–7).

We note that the first beast is pictured as a lion; the second, as a bear; the third, as a leopard; and the fourth as, *"...dreadful and terrible and strong exceedingly."* No animal is found which could properly symbolize this fourth and last world Gentile empire.

The Prophet Daniel was troubled by this vision because he did not understand it. *"I Daniel was grieved in my spirit in the midst of my body, and the visions of my head troubled me.*

"I came near unto one of them that stood by, and asked him the truth of all this. So he told me, and made me know the interpretation of the things" (Daniel 7:15–16).

Then in verse 17, Daniel received a more detailed explanation. Note particularly the fourth one, *"These great beasts, which are four, are four kings, which shall arise out of the earth.*

"But the saints of the most High shall take the kingdom, and possess the kingdom for ever, even for ever and ever.

"Then I would know the truth of the fourth beast, which was diverse from all the others, exceeding dreadful, whose teeth were of iron, and his nails of brass; which devoured, brake in pieces, and stamped the residue with his feet;

"And of the ten horns that were in his head, and of the other which came up, and before whom three fell; even of that horn that had eyes, and a mouth that spake very great things, whose look was more stout than his fellows.

"I beheld, and the same horn made war with the saints, and prevailed against them;

"Until the Ancient of days came, and judgment was given to the saints of the most High; and the time came that the saints possessed the kingdom.

"Thus he said, The fourth beast shall be the fourth kingdom upon earth, which shall be diverse from all kingdoms, and shall devour the whole earth, and shall tread it down, and break it in pieces" (verses 17–23).

Babylon of Gold

Babylon is the first, and it would appear to be the best Gentile world empire, because it is represented by the precious metal, gold, while the next empire is compared to silver. The third empire is pictured as brass, and the last empire is represented by iron. If we were to analyze the development of civilization, however, we most certainly would come to the opposite conclusion. Our democratic government, represented by the iron empire, is no doubt the last one, and there is little room for argument regarding our personal freedom, justice, peace and prosperity. The average person is better off today than during any previous time in history, and what we are experiencing today is unprecedented.

This certainly cannot be said for the Greek, Medo-Persian, or the Babylonian empire. Therefore, we must conclude that the prophetic Word does not speak on a human level of understanding. Why not? Because God's ways are not man's ways. His intentions are revealed in the Scripture, but they must be understood spiritually.

Paul writes in 1st Corinthians 2:10, *"But God hath revealed them unto us by his Spirit: for the Spirit searcheth all things, yea, the deep things of God."*

What, then, is it that God reveals unto us? Answer: The things we perceive with our intellect and consider good may not be good at all from God's point of view! Although we may deem it desirable to live in peace and prosperity with democratic liberties, that does not mean it is good in God's sight.

The first world ruler was, no doubt, a dictator. Yet God calls him "good." The last empire, ruled by a democracy in which the people are in charge and can choose their leader, is shown by God to be the worst type of government in the long run. Our perception of personal liberty, prosperity and peace may well be a case of direct opposition to God's ways!

For example, in the Bible's description of the first world ruler, we read, *"...my servant Nebuchadnezzar, king of Babylon"* (Jeremiah 25:9).

Of Cyrus, King of Persia, we read, *"...Cyrus, He is my shepherd, and shall perform all my pleasure..."* (Isaiah 44:28).

We can't find any similar positive references to the third or the fourth world rulers! Yet, the fourth empire (iron democracy) endues its citizens with more liberty, individual rights, prosperity and peace than all the other systems of government combined. Again, if we only observe these things on an intellectual level, we immediately are confronted with a contradiction: God symbolizes dictatorship by "gold" and democracy by "iron." Therefore, let's take a closer look so we won't miss the point, but, understand God's intention for man.

Liberty Without Discipline

Hebrews 12:6 has this to say, *"For whom the Lord loveth he chasteneth, and scourgeth every son whom he receiveth."* Here, we see the parallel: God disciplines His children. What happens if He doesn't? Verse 8 answers, *"But if ye be without chastisement, whereof all are partakers, then are ye bastards, and not sons."*

The discipline under King Nebuchadnezzar kept the people in line. The laws that were written and signed by the king could not be changed. If the government said, "Thus it shall be," then thus it was! We can see how different the last empire really is in practical ways during elections of government officials under our Roman democratic system. Candidates can promise voters virtually anything, but once elected, they are under no obligation to fulfill those promises.

I think we understand that individual freedom with unlimited liberty can do away with discipline; it allows people to rule themselves according to their own liking. They become rebellious, just as the Apostle Paul prophesied about the endtimes, *"This know also, that in the last days perilous times shall come. For men shall be lovers of their own selves, covetous, boasters, proud, blasphemers, disobedient to parents, unthankful, unholy,*

"Without natural affection, trucebreakers, false accusers, incontinent, fierce, despisers of those that are good,

"Traitors, heady, highminded, lovers of pleasures more than lovers of God" (2nd Timothy 3:1–4).

Hebrews 12:11 tells us how important God's discipline really is, *"Now no chastening for the present seemeth to be joyous, but grievous: nevertheless afterward it yieldeth the peaceable fruit of righteousness unto them which are exercised thereby."* Like it or not, discipline—even when administered by a dictator—is, in the end, the best. Thus, God gave Nebuchadnezzar the gold and us the iron. Note, however, that neither Babylon nor the rest receives an everlasting promise; that is reserved exclusively for Israel.

Babylon or Mystery Babylon?

Babylon, as we will see in this book, has been clearly identified geographically and confirmed archaeologically.

Mystery Babylon, however, is a subject not limited to a geo-graphic region; its scope is world-wide. Therefore, we do well to clearly distinguish between Babylon, the *first* world empire, and Mystery Babylon, the *last* world empire.

Regarding the first Babylon, the Prophet Jeremiah wrote, *"Behold, I am against thee, O destroying mountain, saith the LORD, which destroyest all the earth: and I will stretch out mine hand upon thee, and roll thee down from the rocks, and will make thee a burnt mountain.*

"And they shall not take of thee a stone for a corner, nor a stone for foundations; but thou shalt be desolate for ever, saith the LORD" (Jeremiah 51:25–26). That means final perpetual destruction. Verse 37 confirms, *"And Babylon shall become heaps, a dwellingplace for dragons, an aston-ishment, and an hissing, without an inhabitant."*

The pronouncement of perpetual judgment is emphasized in verses 60–62, *"So Jeremiah wrote in a book all the evil that should come upon Babylon, even all these words that are written against Babylon*

"And Jeremiah said to Seraiah, When thou comest to Babylon, and shalt see, and shalt read all these words;

"Then shalt thou say, O LORD, thou hast spoken against this place, to cut it off, that none shall remain in it, neither man nor beast, but that it shall be desolate for ever." That is the end of Babylon. For approximately 2,500 years, Babylon has not existed, except for a few ruins that have resisted the wind, the sand, the scorching sun and the desert. Just to confirm that Jeremiah 51 is referring to the old Babylon, let's also read the last two verses of this chapter, *"And it shall be, when thou hast made an end of reading this book, that thou shalt bind a stone to it, and cast it into the midst of Euphrates:*

"And thou shalt say, Thus shall Babylon sink, and shall not rise from the evil that I will bring upon her: and they

shall be weary. Thus far are the words of Jeremiah." Note the geographic reference, *"...in the midst of Euphrates."*

Rebuilding Babylon?

Since the rise of Saddam Hussein, many have speculated about the resurrection of the city of Babylon.

In fact, it is assumed that the world headquarters for Mystery Babylon, the last world empire, will be established on the soil of ancient Babylon. I am going to list several reasons why it won't:

No· Peter lived there when he wrote I Peter

1) The city of Babylon has been destroyed and the Bible makes it clear that it shall never rise again.

2) Ancient Babylon does not fit the Bible's specifications for Mystery Babylon, based on Revelation 17 and 18.

   A. The blood of the martyrs of Jesus was never shed in that city (Revelation 17:6).

   B. Ancient Babylon was never built on seven mountains as is required by Scripture (Revelation 17:9).

   C. Ancient Babylon was not built upon the system of religious-political "fornication" as is the case with Mystery Babylon (Revelation 18:3).

   D. Ancient Babylon, when on fire, is not visible from ships on the Mediterranean, *"For in one hour so great riches is come to nought. And every shipmaster, and all the company in ships, and sailors, and as many as trade by sea, stood afar off"* (Revelation 18:17).

3) Present day intellectual resources available to the state of

Iraq (Babylon) are among the lowest in the world. Less than 58% of the country's population over 15 years of age can read and write. Someone has said, "Out of its own national intellect, Iraq would have difficulties producing a bicycle."

Intellect Needed to Lead

Let us elaborate on the above point: When Babylon was leading the world, it was the center of business, knowledge and art. In addition, the laws were made by its leaders.

During the second empire, Medo-Persia, the Medes were in charge of science, technology, the arts, and the military. They ruled the world. Needless to say, any administration must have the power, the money, and the brains to rule such an empire. Uneducated people can't do it.

This can also be said for the third empire, Greece, in which Athens was the center of intellectual power. Even after Greece lost its leadership, it maintained its status as an intellectual center. We read in the New Testament, *"(For all the Athenians and strangers which were there spent their time in nothing else, but either to tell, or to hear some new thing.)"* (Acts 17:21). Greek culture and philosophy is still well entrenched in civilized countries throughout the world.

The center of the fourth Gentile world empire is, indisputably, Rome.

The amazing achievements of the Romans are well documented, even outside the Holy Scriptures. One may travel to Italy today, or for that matter, to most European countries, and find magnificent buildings testifying to the great architectural and engineering skills of the Romans.

We could search the annals of history for a city or nation of equal prominence, and with such an impact on the world, but we would not find one. There is none!

Not only was Rome a glorious world empire 2,000 years ago, but Roman philosophy, culture and law are the foundation of virtually all Western civilized nations.

To reinforce my statement about the Roman influence in the 20th century, here is an article from *Midnight Call*, July 1998, quoting from *Building Design and Construction*, and the prestigious *National Geographic* magazine.

U.S.A.
For May 2000, Pope John Paul Cultural Center in Washington

After a long deliberation, Washington, D.C. has been chosen as the site for the Pope John Paul II Cultural Center, a planned multicultural think tank that will echo the history of the church, but also emphasize its future.

Designed by the Washington office of A/E firm Leo A. Daly, the center is set to be built on land owned by Catholic University of America.

"The materials for the center are traditional, but the design is unapologetically modern," said Al O'Konski, Daly's vice president. The four-story, 100,000–sq. ft. facility will be constructed of limestone, glass, and copper, and include a cornerstone removed from the structure of St. Peter's Basilica in Rome. "We first thought of the center along the lines of a presidential library, but instead designed the structure to appeal to the widest audience possible," he said.

The $51 million project will include three primary components: an intercultural center to host international scholars, a library housing papal writings and encyclicals, and a museum that will feature interactive galleries and computer terminals. The terminals will allow an estimated 750,000 annual users to electronically record what they have learned.

Public spaces will include a children's museum, auditorium and gift shop.

> A contractor for the project will be selected later this month, with construction scheduled to begin this spring. Completion is planned for May 2000.
>
> —Building Design & Construction, March 1998, p.16

A "cornerstone" from St. Peter's Basilica in Rome would perfectly demonstrate America's Roman heritage. To reinforce our statement regarding Roman heritage, here are some excerpts from the American *National Geographic*:

Roman Origins

> "We know that early on, the Romans were ruled by the Etruscans, a powerful nation of central Italy. Chafing under an often brutal monarchy, the leading families of Rome finally overthrew the Etruscan kings—a revolution that would influence, some 2,200 years later, the thinking of Thomas Jefferson and George Washington.
>
> "In the year 244 AUC (that is, 509 B.C.) the patrician families of Rome set up a quasi-representative form of government, with a pair of ruling consuls elected for a one-year term. This marked the beginning of the Roman Republic, a form of government that would continue until Julius Caesar crossed the Rubicon 460 years later. Those five centuries were marked by increasing prosperity and increasing democracy."
>
> —National Geographic, July 1997, p.15

This early democratic system was barely different than ours today. The article continues:

How About "Fat Cat Contributors?"

> "By the second century B.C. the right to vote was so firmly established among the plebeians that Rome developed a vigorous political system—one that would not be unfamiliar to citizens of a modern democracy. There were parties and

A Republic - ruled by laws based upon Scripture
A Democracy- ruled by popular vote
America IS NOT a Democracy 0 Yet 0

factions, fat-cat contributors, banners and billboards, negative advertising, and a pundit class to castigate the pols."

—National Geographic, July 1997, p.21

Just as a modern democracy, the Romans granted rights, but requested duties.

Rights And Duties of Citizens

"Within the broad sweep of uniformity, Roman administration at the local level was flexible, tolerant, and open.

"When Rome conquered a new province, the defeated general and his army were carted away in chains; almost everyone else came out ahead. The local elite were given positions in the Roman hierarchy. Local businesses gained the benefit of Roman roads, water systems, the laws of commerce and the courts. Roman soldiers guarded the town against pirates and marauders. And within a fairly short period, many of the provincial residents would be made cives Romani—citizens of Rome—with all the commensurate rights and duties."

—National Geographic, July 1997, p.30

The Roman Pro-Life movement was actively supported by no one less than Augustus.

Anti-Abortion

"Augustus used all the tools of governing. Concerned about a decline in the birthrate, he employed both the stick (a crackdown on abortion) and the carrot (tax incentives for big families). To see if his policies were effective he took a census of his empire now and then.

"Thus it did in fact come to pass in those days that there went out a decree from Caesar Augustus that all the world should be registered. And just as St. Luke's Gospel tells us, this happened 'when Quirinius was governor of Syria,' in A.D. 6.

Under Roman rule, "world citizenship" was real and prosperity greatest.

Citizen of the World

"History recalls Marcus Aurelius (161–180), the philosopher-king who maintained perspective in the midst of imperial splendor: 'As the Emperor, Rome is my homeland; but as a man, I am a citizen of the world...Asia and Europe are mere dots on the map, the ocean is a drop of water, mighty Mount Athos is a grain of sand in the universe.' Even the cynical Gibbon had to tip his hat: 'If a man were called to fix the period in the history of the world, during which the condition of the human race was most happy and prosperous, he would, without hesitation, name that which elapsed from [A.D. 96 to 180]'—That is, the era of those 'Five Good Emperors.'"

—National Geographic, 7/97, p.35

Without Roman law, today's democracies would not function.

Literacy and Law

"The English historian Peter Salway notes that England under Roman rule had a higher rate of literacy than any British government was able to achieve for the next 14 centuries. One of the most important documentary legacies the Romans left behind was the law—the comprehensive body of statute and case law that some scholars consider our greatest inheritance from ancient Rome.

The ideal of written law as a shield—to protect individuals against one another and against the awesome power of the state—was a concept the Romans took from the Greeks. But it was Rome that put this abstract notion into daily practice, and the practice is today honored around the world."

—National Geographic, August 1997, p.62–63

Ancient Rome was concerned with citizen's liberty.

Innocent Until Proven Guilty

"The emperor Justinian's monumental compilation of the
Digests, the Institutes, and the Revised Code, completed in
A.D. 534, has served as the foundation of Western law ever
since. "Two millennia before the Miranda warnings, the
Romans also established safeguards to assure the rights of
accused criminals. We can see this process at work in the case
against the Christian pioneer St. Paul, as set forth in the New
Testament in the Acts of the Apostles.

"In chapter 22 of Acts, Paul is brought before a Roman
magistrate on criminal charges—apparently for something like
'provoking a riot.' The police are just about to beat and jail him
when Paul pipes up that he is a Roman citizen. That changes
everything, and he is permitted to remain free pending a trial.

"Festus responds, in chapter 25, with a lecture on legal
rights: 'It is not the Roman custom to hand over any man
before he has faced his accusers and has had an opportunity to
defend himself against their charges?'"

—National Geographic, August 1997, p.68

America's democratic system is clearly modeled after the
Roman Republic.

Rome—U.S.A.

"The Roman process of making laws also had a deep influence
on the American system. During the era of the Roman
Republic (509 to 49 B.C.) lawmaking was a bicameral activity. Legislation was first passed by the comitia, the assembly
of the citizens, then approved by the representative of the upper
class, the senate, and issued in the name of the senate and the
people of Rome. Centuries later, when the American Founding
Fathers launched their bold experiment in democratic

government, they took republican Rome as their model. Our laws, too, must go through two legislative bodies. The House of Representatives is our assembly of citizens, and, like its counterpart in ancient Rome, the U.S. Senate was originally designed as a chamber for the elite (it was not until the 17th Amendment, in 1913, that ordinary people were allowed to vote for their senators).

Impressed by the checks and balances of the Roman system, the authors of American government also made sure that an official who violated the law could be "impeached," a word we take from the Roman practice of putting wayward magistrates in pedica.

"The reliance on Roman structures at the birth of the United States was reflected in early American popular culture, which delighted in drawing parallels between U.S. leaders and the noble Romans.

"There was a great vogue for marble statues depicting George Washington, Alexander Hamilton, even Andrew Jackson in Roman attire. A larger-than-life statue of Washington in a toga and sandals is still on exhibit at the National Museum of American History in Washington, D.C."

— National Geographic, August 1997, p. 70

From these historical quotations, we clearly see that Rome, in a real sense, has never ceased to rule the world.

Rome will continue to guide the entire world until the masses are captivated by peace, success, and prosperity under the banner of democracy led by the wicked one, the Antichrist.

Therefore, to find an entity that can fulfill the requirements for the title "Mystery Babylon," we have to look for the richest, most successful system the world has ever known. That is unmistakably Rome or, in modern language, the European Union.

U.S.A.

Someone may now say, "What about the United States of America?" Indeed, the U.S. could qualify as a preliminary candidate for Mystery Babylon because of its great economic, political, military and religious success. For approximately 70 years, the United States was the leader of the Western World. However, America's attempt to reach beyond its borders failed to materialize and ended in the shocking military defeat in Vietnam.

Also, we must add here that the success of the U.S. was primarily due to the import of knowledge from Europe (Rome).

I still vividly recall a daily newspaper in Western Australia which proclaimed in the headlines, "The great British brain drain." That was in 1964!

In the accompanying article, the newspaper reported of over 21,000 top British scientists and engineers leaving the island for America yearly. That trend also applied to other European nations.

What was the reason for the exodus to the U.S.A.? Quite simple: More money! British engineers could earn three times the amount of money in the U.S.A. Successful nations have always tended to harness the "cream of the crop" of other nations for their own benefit.

Bible Facts

To reinforce this statement, let me quote 1st Kings 7:13–14, *"And king Solomon sent and fetched Hiram out of Tyre.*

"He was a widow's son of the tribe of Naphtali, and his father was a man of Tyre, a worker in brass: and he was filled with wisdom, and understanding, and cunning to work all works in brass. And he came to king Solomon, and wrought all his work."

Prosperous King Solomon, the wisest of the kings at that time, imported the best craftsmen from Lebanon! Furthermore, let's also read Daniel 1:3–4, *"And the king spake unto Ashpenaz the master of his eunuchs, that he should bring certain of the children of Israel, and of the king's seed, and of the princes;*

"Children in whom was no blemish, but well favoured, and skilful in all wisdom, and cunning in knowledge, and understanding science, and such as had ability in them to stand in the king's palace, and whom they might teach the learning and the tongue of the Chaldeans."

Thus, we see that success breeds success, or, as another slogan goes, "money makes money." This ancient Biblical philosophy was a major influence on America's success.

However, to answer the question, "Why can't America be 'Mystery Babylon'"? we must answer that the candidate country must meet the four-fold criteria mentioned previously.Therefore, neither the United States, the most successful Roman culturally-based country, nor ancient Babylon can possibly as "Mystery Babylon."

The New Europe

To understand Europe, we must see it from a Biblical perspective with regard to her relationship to Israel. Daniel, the Jew, interpreted the strange dream of Nebuchadnezzar, the first world Gentile ruler.

The interpretation reveals the history of the Gentiles, from the beginning to the end. We have already mentioned this, and will repeat it several more times throughout this book: The last world empire, which is Rome, will continue to exist until the very end.

The last stages of this empire are described in Daniel 2:41–43, *"And whereas thou sawest the feet and toes, part of potters' clay, and part of iron, the kingdom shall be*

divided; but there shall be in it of the strength of the iron,
forasmuch as thou sawest the iron mixed with miry clay.

"And as the toes of the feet were part of iron, and part of
clay, so the kingdom shall be partly strong, and partly
broken.

"And whereas thou sawest iron mixed with miry clay, they
shall mingle themselves with the seed of men: but they shall
not cleave one to another, even as iron is not mixed with
clay."

Most scholars agree that the iron represents Roman
democracy, which for all practical purposes rules today's
political world.

This is reinforced by the reality that never before in history has the world experienced global democracy. Nor has
it been possible to implement such a system world-wide due
to the lack of communication capabilities.

Years ago, the only mode of transportation and communication across the sea was by ship. Sailing from France to
Vietnam, for example, or from Japan to America, would
take many weeks. Today, however, the time it takes to travel
these distances has shrunk to only hours by plane.

And through satellite technology, we have closed the
communication gap to a split second. For the first time in
history, we have created the possibility for a global
society.

Who is the "Clay"?

The "clay" which is mixed with the "iron" (democracy)
represents the Jewish people. They indeed have been
mixed with the nations of the world—including Egypt,
China, America, and the European nations—for over
2,000 years. The Jews have been very successful throughout the world and have established their presence in
notable terms.

They are considered by many to have contributed more to science, art and the intellectual world than any other people. No other group of people or race has been as successful as the Jews. If Jewish achievements in medicine, banking, the arts, engineering, and even agriculture were to be taken away, the world would be much worse today.

One would think that the Jews' contributions to modern science and civilized law would have caused full integration with the Gentiles, but that has not been the case. The Jews have kept their own peculiar identity.

The average American, for example, does not know his roots.

Rarely have I met an American who could say "My roots are in Russia, France, England, Germany, Italy...." But the majority would answer, "I am part Irish, part German, part Spanish, part Polish, part Scottish...."

Thus, we might say that Americans have lost their roots, but gained a new identity. That was expected to happen to the Jews, but it never materialized.

In spite of all their successes, the Jews have kept their identity alive, and in 1948, they founded the State of Israel, the symbol of world Jewish unity.

Israel had been a wasteland, and agriculturally unproductive for about 2,000 years. But today, she has become like the Garden of Eden.

Before the eyes of the world, the Jews changed the topography of the land within just a few years after they took possession of it. It is significant that the other parts of Israel, from the river of Egypt to the river of Euphrates, which presently are almost totally Arab-occupied Israeli territory, have *not* experienced this miraculous change.

When comparing Israel with its neighbors such as Egypt, Jordan, Syria and Lebanon, one can describe those surrounding countries with only three words: poverty, poverty,

poverty! But the Jews who returned from the ends of the world have become a solidified nation. They are speaking Hebrew. They are the most prosperous nation in the Middle East today, and no doubt will one day supercede all others.

So, we see that the Jews mixed with the nations, but never became part of them. The Bible says *"...they shall not cleave one to another..."* (Daniel 2:43). They kept their identity as the clay.

Jeremiah 18:6 declares, *"O house of Israel, cannot I do with you as this potter? saith the LORD. Behold, as the clay is in the potter's hand, so are ye in mine hand, O house of Israel."*

Israel Begins to Mix

Israel is different. She should remain so, but the great tragedy is that Israel does not want to be separated from the other nations. Israel's real sentiment, expressed by her intellectuals and politicians, clearly seems to be that she is just the same as any other nation. Thereby, the first steps are being undertaken for the clay to be mixed with the iron: the Gentile democracy. In all of the Middle East, Israel is the only state with a true Roman democracy.

"We the people" are in charge in Israel. Governments are elected by the people and for the people. Laws are being written by the people and for the people. Because of Israel's initial success, I believe democracy will also be implemented throughout the Middle East and the rest of the world in the near future.

If this is the case—that Israel is being integrated into the Gentile "iron nations"—then we are approaching the time of the end, which will see the fulfillment of the next verse, *"Forasmuch as thou sawest that the stone was cut out of the mountain without hands, and that it brake in pieces the iron, the brass, the clay, the silver, and the gold; the great God*

hath made known to the king what shall come to pass here-
after: and the dream is certain, and the interpretation
thereof sure" (Daniel 2:45). I have deliberately highlighted
Israel in this chapter because Europe (Rome) ruled the
world when the greatest Jew of all times, Jesus, was born,
and Europe must rule again when Jesus comes back.

God chose Israel to rule the world. However, Europe has
ruled the world for over 2,000 years, and the way it looks
today, Europe will continue to be the primary leader. But
only one is destined to lead, and that is Israel. Thus, events
must come to a conclusion sometime in the not-too-distant
future. It is not surprising, for example, that the European
Union is symbolized by its flag of twelve stars in a circle on
blue and the European Constitution declares that twelve
stars will remain, regardless of how many nations will be
admitted into the union.

Clearly, we recognize the imitation of the twelve tribes of
Israel and the twelve apostles of the Lamb!

Someone may now object: "How can you say Europe
ruled the world when only America and Russia attained status as superpowers?" "Superpower status" was primarily
coined by the United States to identify the Soviet Union,
being communist, and the U.S.A., being capitalist.

Since the Soviet Union does not exist any longer, it is natural to assume that the U.S. is the only superpower.
However, I believe that a superpower cannot exist within the
framework of democracy unless the world becomes a mass
democracy, under the leadership of the United Nations, and
thereby create the first true superpower of the world, a
global nation which no doubt is going to exist in the future.
The Bible speaks of world rulership and identifies only four:
Babylon, Medo-Persia, Greece, and Rome. However, the
fourth one, Rome, will merge into the fifth and absolute
final Gentile "superpower." For all practical purposes,

America (North and South) and Australia are European-cultured continents. These nations are the result of European settlement. Americans and Australians not only speak European languages, but their entire intellectual and cultural base originated in Europe.

Looking to the east of Europe, the Asian continent is patterned after European laws and business practices. If Indians want to speak to the Chinese, or the Japanese to the Russians, they have to communicate in a European language. Looking to the south of Europe, we see Africa, where 50% speak French, and almost 40% speak English. There isn't a country in Africa which isn't built upon the intellectual foundation of Europe.

The iron empire (Europe) has dominated the world for over 2,000 years and during the last few decades, it has reemerged even more powerful than ever before in history.

A recent article in our local newspaper, *The State*, reported that foreign firms in the United States are creating five times as many jobs for Americans than American firms. We may not like it, or even believe it, but the facts and figures show clearly that America (North and South) is becoming dependent upon Europe, just as it was in the beginning.

Based on Bible prophecy, the European "iron empire" must spread around the world and solidify all the nations into a global society. Europe is already the richest and most sophisticated continent at this time.

With these facts in mind, we will analyze other entities for consideration for the title, "Mystery Babylon."

Because we are seeing these things come to pass, particularly the integration of Israel into the iron empire, we know that the time is at hand when we should pay close attention to the promise of Luke 21:28, *"And when these things begin to come to pass, then look up, and lift up your heads; for your redemption draweth nigh."*

CHAPTER TWO

Euphrates River in Bible Prophecy

Summary

The Euphrates River is mentioned prominently in the Bible. It is the eastern border of the land God promised to give to Abraham and his descendants through Isaac and Jacob forever. The land is now occupied by Arabs determined to destroy the rightful owners, the Jews, at any costs. This chapter deals with a vital aspect of Babylon.

Psalm 137:1–6, is about the river of Euphrates in the land of Babylon, *"By the rivers of Babylon, there we sat down, yea, we wept, when we remembered Zion.*

"We hanged our harps upon the willows in the midst thereof.

"For there they that carried us away captive required of us a song; and they that wasted us required of us mirth, saying, Sing us one of the songs of Zion.

"How shall we sing the LORD'S song in a strange land?

"If I forget thee, O Jerusalem, let my right hand forget her cunning.

"If I do not remember thee, let my tongue cleave to the roof of my mouth; if I prefer not Jerusalem above my chief joy."

The Jewish Soul And Jerusalem

To better understand this Scripture, we need to stress Israel's situation in the land of Babylon, through which the Euphrates River flows.

Apparently, extreme sadness had taken a hold of the soul of these Jewish people; they refused to be happy. They couldn't sing the songs of Zion in the land of captivity: *"How shall we sing the Lord's song in a strange land?"*

In this Scripture, we see the eternal connection between the Jew and the holy city of Jerusalem: *"...if I prefer not Jerusalem above my chief joy."* Particularly, verses 5 and 6 express the faithfulness of the Jewish people to Jerusalem.

To better understand this statement, let's read it from the Hebrew-English translation, "If I forget you, O Jerusalem, let my right hand wither; let my tongue stick to my palate if I cease to think of you, if I do not keep Jerusalem in memory even at my happiest hour."

What a powerful longing for Jerusalem! Until this very day, Jews still pray "Next year in Jerusalem!"

Righteous Judgment

Another important item to consider in this Psalm is the expression of the wrath upon the enemies of Jerusalem, *"Remember, O LORD, the children of Edom in the day of Jerusalem; who said, Rase it, rase it, even to the foundation thereof.*

"O daughter of Babylon, who art to be destroyed; happy shall he be, that rewardeth thee as thou hast served us.

"Happy shall he be, that taketh and dasheth thy little ones against the stones" (verses 7–9).

As far as our sense of judgment is concerned, we would find this to be an excessive statement: *"...dasheth thy little ones against the stones."*

I have to admit that I can't fully understand that statement. But, I do know that God's judgments are righteous. Only when we're convinced of our own wretchedness in contrast to His perfect righteousness and understand God's great love as expressed in His gift of sending His only begotten Son to die on Calvary's cross, will we begin to understand the requirement for total judgment.

The Sinless One Judged

What could be more cruel than to take a person who never did anything wrong, who never harmed anyone, who blessed and healed people, who restored the sight of the blind and the hearing of the deaf, and who even raised the dead to life, to take Him and nail Him to the cross?

This greatest benefactor to humanity was taken and brutally beaten, then crucified with the planned purpose of having Him bleed to death. If only we can begin to understand God's righteousness, then we'll understand our hopeless position in relationship to a perfect and Holy God.

These facts are important for us to keep in mind when we speak about the prophetic meaning of the Euphrates River.

[handwritten margin note: descendents of Esau. lived in area of Petra to Elat & the Arava]

Prophecy is the Word of God and the Word of God is identified as a person, *"In the beginning was the Word, and the Word was with God, and the Word was God"* (John 1:1). However, before the Word became flesh and dwelt among us, the Euphrates River already played a major role in that it was named in relation to paradise. In this chapter, we'll see how this river is still important for the church, Israel, and the world.

Israel's Beginning at the Euphrates
Abraham, from whom Israel originates, came from the other side of the Euphrates River. In Joshua 24:2–3, we read the following, *"...Your fathers dwelt on the other side of the flood* [Euphrates] *in old time, even Terah, the father of Abraham, and the father of Nachor: and they served other gods. And I took your father Abraham from the other side of the flood, and led him throughout all the land of Canaan, and multiplied his seed, and gave him Isaac."*

It's evident from this Scripture, therefore, that Abraham, the beginning of Israel, originates with the Gentiles. The Euphrates is often mentioned as being "the flood," because during the rainy season this important river would flood much of the land.

Later in history, the first martyr, Stephen, when he was accused of angering the people, testified, *"...Men, brethren, and fathers, hearken; The God of glory appeared unto our father Abraham, when he was in Mesopotamia, before he dwelt in Charran"* (Acts 7:2). Mesopotamia refers to the northern part of today's Syria and Iraq. This, therefore, relates to Abraham. The Euphrates, which is first mentioned in Genesis 2:14, is also the border of paradise: *"And the name of the third river is Hiddekel: that is it which goeth toward the east of Assyria. And the fourth river is Euphrates."*

Abraham's Conversion

As we've just pointed out, Abraham's past belongs to the heathen, those who worship idols, the Bible tells us. Therefore, Abraham had to be changed; he had to be turned around, taken out of one place and transferred into another. He had to experience a conversion.

Let's discuss Abraham's calling, his success and failures in more detail. Abraham's conversion is based on God's calling, *"Now the LORD had said unto Abram, Get thee out of thy country, and from thy kindred, and from thy father's house, unto a land that I will shew thee"* (Genesis 12:1).

We've already seen that God reaches His goals through segregation, not integration, as was the case in Genesis 11 where the people united to build a tower which would reach unto heaven. The people who built the Tower of Babel acted contrary to the will of God.

Abraham, however, did the will of God, *"So Abram departed, as the Lord had spoken unto him"* (verse 4).

Abraham the Syrian

Abraham wasn't in the truest sense an Israeli; he was a Syrian. He had to change his citizenship, too.

Today's Syria is Israel's most bitter enemy. Why? Because it is the closest relative to Israel.

Abraham's brother is called a Syrian. Isaac's wife was also a Syrian, *"...the daughter of Bethuel the Syrian of Padanaram, the sister to Laban the Syrian"* (Genesis 25:20).

Later, Isaac's son Jacob took Rebekah as his wife, whose father was *"...Laban, son of Bethuel the Syrian, the brother of Rebekah, Jacob's and Esau's mother"* (Genesis 28:5).

Moses admonishes the children of Israel to recognize their roots: *"...thou shalt speak and say before the Lord thy God, A Syrian ready to perish was my father, and he went down into Egypt, and sojourned there..."* (Deuteronomy 26:5). That's a confession the Israelites had to make to remind them where they came from!

You Must be Converted

For all useful purposes, we can say Abraham was a Gentile; he had to cross over; he had to be converted.

The Apostle Paul, thousands of years after Abraham's departure, wrote in 2nd Corinthians 5:17, *"Therefore if any man be in Christ, he is a new creature: old things are passed away; behold, all things are become new."*

The question we need to ask ourselves repeatedly is, "Have old things really passed away?" Remember the old life you lived before you were born-again of the Spirit of God? Are any of the old tendencies and characteristics visible in your new life? They must disappear, surrendered into the death of Jesus Christ!

The account of Abraham shows us that to follow God's plan, we must change our direction. Every unredeemed person in the world is by nature going in the wrong direction, which leads to destruction, and finally hell, ending in the "lake of fire." What must you do to end up in hell? Answer: You don't have to do anything. You're automatically going to hell because of what you are, an unforgiven sinner without Jesus. The Bible says all have sinned. There is no righteous one, no not one. Isaiah 64:6 proclaims: *"But we are all as an unclean thing, and all our righteousnesses are as filthy rags; and we all do fade as a leaf; and our iniquities, like the wind, have taken us away."*

There's no such thing as a righteous person, no matter how good he may appear, how well he may camouflage himself. The only righteousness that counts before God is the righteousness which we receive free through faith in Jesus!

First Murder

We have already learned that paradise was found in the geographic vicinity of the Euphrates. But in this area, the first murder recorded for us in the Bible happened. It is documented for us in Genesis 4:8, *"And Cain talked with Abel his brother: and it came to pass, when they were in the field, that Cain rose up against Abel his brother, and slew him."*

Since then, men have been murdering each other. Based on Scripture, this won't end until the Prince of Peace comes!

First Ecumenical Dialogue

It is meaningful that the first murder was a result of the first ecumenical dialogue: The two brothers had a religious discussion! The Bible doesn't report the content of it, but no doubt, it must have been of a religious nature. But, we do know that the result was a murder. The offering of Abel was acceptable unto the Lord, but not the offering of Cain.

From the preceding verses in Genesis 4, we learn that both Abel and Cain did their normal day-to-day chores. They had to work hard to make a living. But, there was a distinct difference between these two brothers. Cain brought an offering of the fruit of the ground while Abel sacrificed "the firstlings of his flock." In Abel's case, blood was shed for the remission of sin. Hebrews 9:22 states, *"...without shedding of blood is no remission."*

Unity at the Cost of Truth

As it was in the beginning of humanity, when an ecumenical dialogue ended in murder, so it is today, in the endtimes. Religious dialogues are happening the world over. If two diverse religions "worship" together, they make headlines in the news media. It is considered "politically correct" and called "great progress." A newspaper article had this to report:

Scholar Attempts to Relate Zen, Taoism to Christianity

Two lectures intended to relate Zen and Taoism to Christianity and Western education will be presented at the University of South Carolina.

Dr. Kwang-ming Wu will be the guest lecturer. Wu is the author of eight books on Chinese thought and Taoism. He has taught at Yale, the University of Wisconsin and the National Chung Cheng University in Taiwan. Wu will speak on "Zen-Christian Manifestation of God: A Zen Deepening of Christian Understanding... learning as a Master from the Master: Chuang Tzu the Taoist in University Education."

—The State, 1/22/98, p.B-3

The Bible doesn't leave us in the dark about what will happen to man's attempts at religious ecumenism. It will lead to the greatest disaster the world has ever known!

Just as Cain and Abel's dialogue didn't lead to peace, the World Council of Churches and many other ecumenical groups and their work won't bring peace; their efforts are doomed to fail.

Incidentally, all unity-seeking religious organizations will also fail. Why? Because real peace and unity have already been established by our Lord Jesus Christ on Calvary's cross when He cried out, "It is finished!"

Euphrates Today

Today, almost 6,000 years after the murder of Abel, bloodshed is continuing in that very place, right there near the Euphrates River. Even in recent history, starting in 1980, war between Iran and Iraq took place; an eight-year war which cost up to a million human lives, many of them children. "Why," we may ask, "is the Euphrates River so important?" Because this river is the eastern border of the

Promised Land. In verse 18 of Genesis 15, we read, *"In the same day the Lord made a covenant with Abram, saying, Unto thy seed have I given this land, from the river of Egypt unto the great river, the river Euphrates."*

Clearly, God had already given this land, from the Euphrates River to the river of Egypt, to Abraham long before the nation of Israel even existed. This land was promised once and for all, and that promise has never been withdrawn. Abraham is the beginning of Israel, and God promised that he would be the beginning of a people, out of which would come forth the Savior. To Abraham, God said, *"...in thee shall all families of the Earth be blessed"* (Genesis 12:3).

To Abraham's son Isaac, God promised, *"...in thy seed shall all the nations of the Earth be blessed"* (Gen. 26:4).

The same promise was passed on to Isaac's son Jacob, *"...in thy seed shall all the families of the Earth be blessed"* (Genesis 28:14).

Euphrates River, the Biblical Border

Today, archaeologists debate whether Israel ever took possession of the Promised Land up to the Euphrates River. Let archaeologists and liberal theologians debate as long as they want. The Bible tells us very plainly that the northern border of Israel is the Euphrates River. In 2nd Samuel 8:3, we read, *"David smote also Hadadezer, the son of Rehob, king of Zobah, as he went to recover his border at the river Euphrates."*

Not only do we read here that David conquered the land up to the Euphrates River, but that he *recovered* it. You can't recover something that doesn't belong to you in the first place!

Therefore, the Euphrates has great meaning. It separates God's land from the world's land.

It also spiritually separates Jerusalem from Babylon. These two cities are diametrically opposed to each other. From Babylon comes the false peace, but from Jerusalem comes real peace!

Babylon Represents Rebellion
The Babylonian territory, on the other side of the Euphrates River, is a picture of rebellion. This was clearly exhibited when men built the Tower of Babel. It became a manifestation of visible rebellion against the living God. Two things become apparent:

1) The Tower of Babel is the symbol of self-redemption.

2) The building of the Tower of Babel represents people power (democracy) in action.

It is significant that the Bible doesn't mention a certain king, a dictator, or strong leader who brought the people together. Rather, *"And they said one to another, Go to, let us make brick, and burn them thoroughly. And they had brick for stone, and slime had they for mortar.*
"And they said, Go to, let us build us a city and a tower, whose top may reach unto heaven; and let us make us a name, lest we be scattered abroad upon the face of the whole Earth" (Genesis 11:3–4).
Have you noticed the words "they," "us," and "we"? "We the people" will produce unity, prosperity, and salvation! Note also the direction the people were headed:
The Babylonians attempted to 'reach unto heaven' with their tower.
That is typical for man; he thinks he can redeem himself. Salvation, however, works in the opposite direction: not from Earth to heaven, but from heaven to Earth!

Who Are We?

As believers in the Lord Jesus Christ, we need to reanalyze our position we are in right now and where we have come from. It is good for us to confess before the Father in heaven who we were before our conversion. The Apostle Paul reminds us about our past, *"Know ye not that the unrighteous shall not inherit the kingdom of God? Be not deceived: neither fornicators, nor idolaters, nor adulterers, nor effeminate, nor abusers of themselves with mankind. Nor thieves, nor covetous, nor drunkards, nor revilers, nor extortioners, shall inherit the kingdom of God. And such were some of you."* This clearly exposes our past.

However, the Scripture continues, *"...but ye are washed, but ye are sanctified, but ye are justified in the name of the Lord Jesus, and by the Spirit of our God"* (1st Corinthians 6:9–11). We should acknowledge who we have been in times past and who we have become through His grace. We are washed in the blood of the Lamb. He has cleansed us from all of our iniquities, and we're now children of God on our way to heaven. Isn't that wonderful?

Abraham's Brother

Let's take a look at Abraham's brother. In Genesis 22:20–21 we read, *"And it came to pass after these things, that it was told Abraham, saying, Behold, Milcah, she hath also born children unto thy brother Nahor; Huz his firstborn, and Buz his brother, and Kemuel the father of Aram."*

Here's what *Unger's Bible Dictionary* tells us about Aram:

> "Aram-Naharaim, Aram of the (Two) Rivers," was the country between the Tigris and Euphrates (Greek, Mesopotamia) or more probably the territory between the Euphrates and the Habur. This was the region of Haran where the Aramaeans had settled in patriarchal times, where Abraham sojourned, and from which Aramaean power spread."

Syria was once a great empire from about 1,000 B.C. to 625 B.C. It ruled all the orient for about 375 years. Egypt and Israel were under Syrian rule formerly, and Syria, a great empire from about 1,000 B.C. to 625 B.C., ruled all the Orient during those 375 years. Abraham's family originates from near the Euphrates River.

Syria Occupies Israel's Territory

When we take a look at the map of the old Syrian Empire, we see Judah and Jerusalem standing like two tiny islands. Only Judah could resist the Syrians.

Today's Syria no longer occupies that territory, however. But, it still holds on to parts of the Promised Land. In the future, Syria will have to return these parts of the Promised Land to Israel, the rightful owner.

All the political agreements we're hearing about in the media are only of temporary value.

No matter whether it's the Camp David Peace treaty, the Oslo peace process, or any other document that has been signed formerly or will be signed eventually, they're only temporal; they will not last.

Why? Because they don't recognize God's boundaries for the Promised Land!

Lebanon Occupies Israeli Territory

God's promise to Abraham continued to the fathers and was passed on to Joshua, who entered Israel. He led the people through the Jordan River and victoriously conquered the land under the direction of the Lord.

In Joshua 1:4 we read, *"From the wilderness and this Lebanon even unto the great river, the river Euphrates, all the land of the Hittites, and unto the great sea toward the going down of the sun, shall be your coast."* Joshua received the clear commandment to divide the land for an inheritance to the twelve tribes, *"All the inhabitants of the hill country from Lebanon unto Misrephothmaim, and all the Sidonians, them will I drive out from before the children of Israel: only divide thou it by lot unto the Israelites for an inheritance, as I have commanded thee"* (Joshua 13:6).

The Natural Border: Euphrates

Now that we've established Israel's border on the Euphrates River, let's take a closer look at this so-called "hot spot of the world," where the Euphrates flows until this day.

The source of the river is to be found in Turkey, from where it runs south through much of Syria, then through the lengths of Iraq.

The approximate total length of the river is 2,800 KM (1,740 miles).

For Israel, the Euphrates River is a natural protection from the Far East nations.

To reach Israel by land from China, India, or Japan, they would have to go through parts of Russia, Pakistan, Afghanistan, and Iran, then over the mountains of Turkey to Israel.

The optional and easy way is to cross the Euphrates River. Not only is Israel protected from the northeast by the Euphrates, but is also protected from the east and south by desert, and in the west, by the Mediterranean.

Based on these facts, one would think that Israel is safe and secure from all neighboring enemies.

That isn't the case and never has been. There have always been nations, even until this day, who oppose this tiny country. The reason is twofold:

1) When Israel was obedient to God and followed His commandments, the blessing of the Lord came upon the land and Israel became the envy of the surrounding nations.

2) Behind the wrath and the hatred of the enemies stands the father of lies, the Devil. He works in the invisible world provoking those who are in darkness to fight against the Light.

Egypt

When writing about the Euphrates River, we must stress that we're not only concerned with geographic areas, but as we've already seen in Abraham's case, with people as well. For that reason, let's look at some of Israel's bitter enemies.

When Israel was born as a nation, we saw the wrath of the evil one turning against them. Pharaoh, who ruled the land of Egypt, recognized that the blessings of God were upon these people. He became afraid that they would have the upper hand one day.

Pharaoh apparently didn't know that Canaan was Israel's land, and therefore the Hebrews were no threat to Egypt. But, that's how the enemy always works: He uses parts of the truth to camouflage his lie!

All Pharaoh could see and understand was that Israel was *"...fruitful, and increased abundantly, and multiplied, and waxed exceeding mighty; and the land was filled with them"* (Exodus 1:7).

When a new king who did not know Joseph ascended to the throne of Egypt, *"...he said unto his people, Behold, the people of the children of Israel are more and mightier than we: Come on, let us deal wisely with them; lest they multiply, and it come to pass, that, when there falleth out any war, they join also unto our enemies, and fight against us, and so get them up out of the land"* (Exodus 1:9–10).

This false alarm, the message the father of lies whispered in Pharaoh's ears, didn't decrease the blessing upon Israel. The opposite became true, *"But the more they afflicted them, the more they multiplied and grew. And they were grieved because of the children of Israel"* (verse 12).

Church Persecuted

We have a parallel here, found in the church. In Acts chapter 4, we read about the religious authorities forbidding the preaching of the Gospel, *"...let us straitly threaten them, that they speak henceforth to no man in this name"* (Acts 4:17).

The believers in Jerusalem started a prayer meeting, and we read about the result that followed, *"And when they had prayed, the place was shaken where they were assembled together; and they were all filled with the Holy Ghost, and they spake the Word of God with boldness.*

"And with great power gave the apostles witness of the resurrection of the Lord Jesus: and great grace was upon them all" (verse 31;33).

Persecution, particularly through the leadership of Saul, was carried out against the churches, as we read in Acts 8:3, *"As for Saul, he made havoc of the church, entering into every house, and haling* [following] *men and women committed them to prison."*

Verse 4 tells us, *"Therefore they that were scattered abroad went every where preaching the word."*

Church Not Political

I believe we have a mystery shown in these and other Scriptures which relates to the action of the true church and today's "churchianity."

The Church of Jesus Christ knows that it is *in* the world but not *of* the world. Our task is distinctively different from the world, because we're not a permanent part of it. For that reason, we don't have the authority to change the government God has installed. We all know that all governments are put into office by God and taken out of office by God.

I hadn't looked at it like this before.

He is in control of all things. When reading the New Testament, particularly the Acts of the Apostles, we don't read of the Christians organizing themselves in opposition to any government, but what they did was fulfill the Lord's command, and that is "preach the Gospel." In contrast, today, churchianity has become a strong political force to be reckoned with. These activists say, "We want our rights! We refuse to be accused falsely, mistreated, and we're willing to spend our time, energy and money to fight on the political level!"

Such political activity is advantageous and wonderful for religions, but we find no proof in the Scripture that such activity helps or contributes to the body of Christ.

However, we clearly see that "Christianity" is mixing with "churchianity," which we know will lead to the full integration with "Mystery Babylon" in the end.

Genocide Conspiracy

Now, let's return to our analysis of Egypt: Pharaoh took it upon himself to execute a plan of genocide against Israel, *"The king of Egypt spake to the Hebrew midwives, of which the name of the one was Shiphrah, and the name of the other Puah: And he said,*

"When ye do the office of a midwife to the Hebrew women, and see them upon the stools; if it be a son, then ye shall kill him: but if it be a daughter, then she shall live" (Exodus 1:15–16).

This was obviously a secret mission. The Egyptian leader wanted to end the imagined threat, but he failed again because *"...the midwives feared God, and did not as the king of Egypt commanded them, but saved the men children alive"* (verse 17). When we study the king of Egypt and his deeds, we quickly notice how one sin led to another. In the beginning, the danger was only imagined. Had he read history, Pharaoh most likely wouldn't have dealt with Israel as he did. He should have known that the land of Canaan—not the land of Egypt—had been given to the Israelites by the God of Abraham, Isaac, and Jacob.

Genocide, a National Policy

After repeated failure at quietly killing off the male children of the Hebrews, the king of Egypt became openly hostile and commanded genocide, *"And Pharaoh charged all his people, saying, Every son that is born ye shall cast into the river, and every daughter ye shall save alive"* (Exodus 1:22).

If Pharaoh had destroyed Israel, God couldn't have brought forth the Savior from the seed of Abraham and would have had to admit defeat. But, God is faithful and will bring to pass the fulfillment of all promises. Pharaoh failed and Israel moved out of bondage victoriously!

Haman, the Enemy of the Jews

About a thousand years after Israel's slavery in Egypt, we see another wicked plot by another one of Satan's servants to eliminate the nation. King Ahasuerus, who reigned over his world empire, *"...from India even unto Ethiopia..."* (Esther 1:1) promoted Haman, *"...and advanced him, and set his seat above all the princes that were with him"* (Esther 3:1).

This man didn't perceive a threat from the Jewish people, but on one occasion his pride was hurt because a certain Jew by the name of Mordecai didn't bow down in reverence before him. Hence, Haman was *"...full of wrath."*

This is understandable to a certain degree. Many leaders before and after Haman had been "full of wrath." They persecuted many people of other races or tribes throughout history. But, Haman's wrath was more intense.

Satan obviously recognized that he had found a willing tool to do his bidding. Esther 3:6 reads, *"And he* [Haman] *thought scorn to lay hands on Mordecai alone; for they had shewed him the people of Mordecai: wherefore Haman sought to destroy all the Jews that were throughout the whole kingdom of Ahasuerus, even the people of Mordecai."*

That truly reflects someone "full of wrath." Because one man hadn't honored him, Haman permitted his fury to grow so that genocide of the Jewish people would be the only way to satisfy his hurt pride!

Haman Knew the Jews

Obviously this man knew the Jews. He must have known that they were God's chosen people. Surely, he must have heard that the Messiah would one day come from these people and redeem humanity.

How do we know that? Answer: Where Haman talks to King Ahasuerus, and says, *"...their* (Jews) *laws are diverse from all people; neither keep they the king's laws: therefore, it is not for the king's profit to suffer them"* (Esther 3:8).

There is some truth in that statement. The Jews were "diverse"; they were different, but they were definitely not a liability to the king! Lies quickly took root in his heart and led him to the most disastrous decision. Pharaoh of Egypt planned to decrease the strength of Israel, but Haman planned to wipe out the whole Jewish race!

Haman's Conspiracy

Surely, the Devil must have danced with joy when he found such a man willing to be diabolically inspired to proceed with a plan to exterminate God's chosen people. Haman presented his clever plan to the king, *"If it please the king, let it be written that they may be destroyed: and I will pay ten thousand talents of silver to the hands of those that have the charge of the business, to bring it into the king's treasuries.*

"And the king took his ring from his hand, and gave it unto Haman the son of Hammedatha the Agagite, the Jews' enemy" (Esther 3:9–10).

Haman failed to recognize that the God of Israel doesn't sleep. A plan of salvation for God's people had already been prepared!

Haman's Embarrassment

Haman should have known that his end was already sealed when an embarrassment came his way. One night, the king couldn't sleep. He apparently had nothing else to do, so he read the records that were written and noticed that a Jew by the name of Mordecai hadn't been rewarded for his heroic act.

Here's how it happened: *"On that night could not the king sleep, and he commanded to bring the book of records of the chronicles; and they were read before the king.*

"And it was found written, that Mordecai had told of Bigthana and Teresh, two of the king's chamberlains, the keepers of the door, who sought to lay hand on the king Ahasuerus.

"And the king said, What honour and dignity hath been done to Mordecai for this? Then said the king's servants that ministered unto him, There is nothing done for him" (Esther 6:1–3).

This illustrates the importance of reading the Scriptures. The Bible is the guideline for believers, the light on our path so we won't go astray. We need to read it, from Genesis to Revelation, 365 days a year. When we do so, we'll be familiar with God's plan for His people and the world. But, when we neglect to read His priceless Word, we can easily fall into the trap of Satan! We already mentioned that if Pharaoh had read recorded history, he would have known that an Israelite by the name of Joseph was the savior of Egypt and had made the house of Pharaoh rich. But, he had failed to read the Chronicles, therefore, he wasn't informed, and was led astray by the cunning devices of Satan.

No doubt, it was God's providence that the king couldn't sleep on that night.

Someone else, however, couldn't sleep either, and that was Haman. He was so sure of victory that he apparently made much noise, so the king asked, *"Who is in the court?"* It was Haman, *"...Now Haman was come into the outward court of the king's house, to speak unto the king to hang Mordecai on the gallows that he had prepared for him"* (Esther 6:4).

In answer to the inquiry, the king's servants said, *"...Behold, Haman standeth in the court. And the king said, Let him come in"* (verse 5).

Haman went to the king. Now the king asked him, *"What should be done to the man whom the king wished to honor?"*

Full of pride, Haman couldn't think of anyone but himself. He proposed in elaborate detail how that man should be honored. Obviously, he was thinking that he was the one to be honored!

Then came the great shocker, *"...Make haste, and take the apparel and the horse, as thou hast said, and do even so to Mordecai the Jew, that sitteth at the king's gate: let nothing fail of all that thou hast spoken"* (Esther 6:10).

Quite apparently, hate makes one blind. When Haman went home, he still didn't fully recognize his fate. But his friends, even his wife, knew. Haman's advisors said, *"...If Mordecai be of the seed of the Jews before whom thou has began to fall, thou shall not prevail against him, but shalt surely fall before him"* (Esther 6:13).

Haman Exposed

Meanwhile, God's plan was in full progress. The queen had made a risky decision to approach the king without permission. She stated, *"If I perish, I perish."*

After the king extended his grace, Esther responded, *"...If I have found favor in thy sight, O king, and if it please the king, let my life be given me at my petition, and my people at my request: For we are sold, I and my people, to be destroyed, to be slain, and to perish. But if we had been sold for bondmen and bondwomen, I had held my tongue, although the enemy could not countervail the king's damage"* (Esther 7:3–4).

This was unthinkable for the king to understand. Full of wrath, he asked, *"...Who is he, and where is he, that durst presume in his heart to do so?"* She answered, *"...The adversary and enemy is this wicked Haman. Then Haman was afraid before the king and the queen"* (verse 6).

The result of the plot to eliminate the Jews is described in verse 10, *"So they hanged Haman on the gallows that he had prepared for Mordecai. Then was the king's wrath pacified."*

Just as Pharaoh, who had planned to drown all the Jewish male children in the water, drowned in the Red Sea, Haman was hung on the very gallows on which he had planned to hang Mordecai!

The Unchangeable Law

But there's more to this important story. With his ring, the king had already sealed the death sentence on all Jewish people in his empire. This law couldn't be changed.

This is highly interesting because, in our day, under the democratic system, everything can be changed. Politicians can promise, as they often do, things that sound good to potential voters.

But, when they're elected, politicians don't have to keep any of their promises. Even laws which are still on the books are being invalidated by not being enforced.

Such a reversal was impossible in the Persian kingdom, even with a powerful ruler like King Ahasuerus. The law couldn't be abolished. But, an alternative law wouldn't violate the existing one.

A new law had to be signed and sealed, *"Wherein the king granted the Jews which were in every city to gather themselves together, and to stand for their life, to destroy, to slay, and to cause to perish, all the power of the people and province that would assault them, both little ones and women, and to take the spoil of them for a prey"* (Esther 8:11).

This writing was spread in haste throughout the kingdom, *"The copy of the writing for a commandment to be given in every province was published unto all people, and that the Jews should be ready against that day to avenge themselves on their enemies"* (verse 13).

The Jews' Salvation

What was the result? *"The Jews gathered themselves together in their cities throughout all the provinces of the king Ahasuerus, to lay hand on such as sought their hurt: and no man could withstand them; for the fear of them fell upon all people"* (Esther 9:2).

Instead of destroying the Jews, Haman's plot made them stronger than ever before.

Many of the Gentiles then wanted to become Jews, *"And in every province, and in every city, whithersoever the king's commandment and his decree came, the Jews had joy and gladness, a feast and a good day. And many of the people of the land became Jews; for the fear of the Jews fell upon them"* (Esther 8:17).

Hitler — Holocaust

The most murderous campaign ever undertaken in history happened during Hitler's 12 year reign over Germany. He was responsible for the murder of more than six million Jews as he tried to solve "the Jewish problem" once and for all.

One tool the infamous leader used was poison gas. He then had victim's bodies disposed of by fire. It's not surprising that this diabolically-inspired man met the same fate: His body was doused with petrol and set on fire!

God's Eternal Promises

I'm emphasizing these three examples to show that the Jews are a unique people. Never must any people so arrogantly think that they're somehow equal to Israel.

Neither the United Nations, the European Union, the United States, nor any other entity is capable of changing God's eternal resolution. He has given the Jews unconditional promises which He'll fulfill. The Promised Land, from the river of Egypt to the great Euphrates River is the God-given property of the Jewish people for eternity! And, Jerusalem is Israel's capital city forever!

Jeremiah–Babylon

The Jews are indestructible and so is the land because their existence is based on the eternal promises of God. The Prophet Jeremiah mentions this fact in chapter 31, *"Thus saith the LORD, which giveth the sun for a light by day, and the ordinances of the moon and of the stars for a light by night, which divideth the sea when the waves thereof roar; The LORD of hosts is his name:*

"If those ordinances depart from before me, saith the LORD, then the seed of Israel also shall cease from being a nation before me for ever" (verses 35–36).

This same prophet speaks also about the end of Babylon in chapter 51 where the word "Babylon" appears 36 times. He received clear instruction from the Lord:

"...when thou hast made an end of reading this book, that thou shalt bind a stone to it, and cast it into the midst of Euphrates:

"And thou shalt say, Thus shall Babylon sink, and shall not rise from the evil that I will bring upon her: and they shall be weary. Thus far are the words of Jeremiah" (Jeremiah 51:63–64).

It's important to understand here that Babylon is the beginning of the times of the Gentiles, and Mystery Babylon is the final stage of the Gentile world power structure. Between these two lies the empire of Medo-Persia, Greece and Rome.

The above Scripture (Jeremiah 51) has been fulfilled. Babylon sunk, never arose, and never will rise again. But the spirit of Babylon, comprising rebellion against God, and rebellion against the Lord Jesus Christ, is a frightful reality which is becoming more visible in our day.

During the Babylonian kingdom and those following, Medo-Persia, Greece and Rome, the establishment of a one-world religion was nearly impossible. But, during the final world empire of Mystery Babylon, this is becoming a reality.

Judgment at the Euphrates

In the Book of Jeremiah, we read the prophecy of the coming final battle when God's wrath will be poured upon the Gentile nations, who will collectively oppose the Jews with the aim of destroying them. *"For this is the day of the Lord GOD of hosts, a day of vengeance, that he may avenge him of his adversaries: and the sword shall devour, and it shall be satiate and made drunk with their blood: for the Lord*

[handwritten in margin: Is Mystery Babylon is the geographical Babylon, one is the same ??.]

GOD of hosts hath a sacrifice in the north country by the river Euphrates" (Jeremiah 46:10).

We see again that the Euphrates plays a major role geographically at this great battle. These judgments are sure to come because the nations of the world will have turned against Israel for the very last time.

Jerusalem: Cup of Trembling

Today, we're already witnessing the beginning of a conflict that no man can solve: Jerusalem. Read the words of Zechariah the prophet, *"The burden of the word of the Lord for Israel, saith the Lord, which stretcheth forth the heavens, and layeth the foundation of the Earth, and formeth the spirit of man within him. Behold, I will make Jerusalem a cup of trembling unto all the people round about, when they shall be in the siege both against Judah and against Jerusalem.*

"And in that day will I make Jerusalem a burdensome stone for all people: all that burden themselves with it shall be cut in pieces, though all the people of the Earth be gathered together against it" (Zechariah 12:1–3).

Someone may now object and say, "Well, this has already taken place. The Romans destroyed Jerusalem and the Temple in A.D. 70." That's true, but here we're specifically told that this last conflict involves *"...all the people of the Earth...,"* not just the Romans. We know that not all this prophecy was fulfilled then.

Nations Oppose Jewish Jerusalem

Even today, we're witnesses of the fact that no nation favors Israel's unconditional possession of Jerusalem and the Holy Land. Even neutral nations such as Switzerland follow in the footsteps of the United Nations which opposes the Jews by saying, "No" to Jerusalem and "No" to Israel's possession of the entire Promised Land. Almost daily, the media reports of continuous negotiations to make Jerusalem an international city.

"Under no circumstances must this city be exclusively Jewish," some insist.

This shouldn't surprise us, for the Lord says, *"I will gather all nations against Jerusalem to battle."*

Israel's Salvation

How, then, will Israel escape? There's only one escape, one type of salvation, and that's through the Lord Jesus Christ. Zechariah proclaims, *"...his feet shall stand in that day upon the Mount of Olives which is before Jerusalem on the east..."* (Zechariah 14:4).

Salvation won't come through the power of weapons of war, but it will come through His Spirit, *"...I will pour out upon the house of David, and upon the inhabitants of Jerusalem, the spirit of grace and of supplications:*

"And they shall look upon me whom they have pierced, and they shall mourn for him, as one mourneth for his only son, and shall be in bitterness for him, as one that is in bitterness for his firstborn" (Zechariah 12:10).

Only Jesus Saves

We understand that Israel brought forth the Savior of the world. This has already happened. Jesus came, and He clearly stated, *"Salvation is of the Jews."*

The Lion of the tribe of Judah isn't only the answer for Israel and the world, but Jesus is the Savior of each individual who trusts Him for the forgiveness of sin and receives eternal life. John 3:36 states,

"He that believeth on the Son hath everlasting life: and he that believeth not the Son shall not see life; but the wrath of God abideth on him."

Final Judgment of the Euphrates

We read the name "Euphrates" for the last time in the Bible in Revelation 16:12. After five terrible vials of wrath have come upon humanity, we see neither faith nor repentance; rather, we read that they, *"...blasphemed the God of heaven because of their pains and their sores, and repented not of their deeds"* (Revelation 16:11). Then in verse 12, we see the Far East nations marching to little Israel for the Battle of Armageddon, *"And the sixth angel poured out his vial upon the great river Euphrates; and the water thereof was dried up, that the way of the kings of the east might be prepared."*

To summarize, the Euphrates River which flows through the land of Babylon (Iraq) will continue to be in the headlines until the last battle.

Not only recently have we seen the land of the Euphrates involved in military conflict, but this has taken place now for several decades. By this, we understand that we're approaching the conclusion of world events, and therefore, the Rapture can't be too far off!

We must stress here that the events which have happened in history in the geographic area of the Euphrates River were never truly international, until recently. This was vividly shown to the whole world during the Gulf conflict in 1991. Virtually the whole world gathered against the aggressor Saddam Hussein, the ruler of Babylon (Iraq).

I can't stress this enough: We're living in the last stages of the endtimes!

Finally, a world religion is being formed. We must emphasize that all movements which try to unify religions—whether they originate with the Vatican, Buddhism, Hinduism, Islam, or fundamental Christianity—will only achieve temporary success. In the end, this one-world religion will lead to the greatest disaster the world has ever known.

Therefore, dear friend, be sure that you are on the winning side. You must know the Lord Jesus Christ as your personal Savior. He may come sooner than we think!

The present-day events and Biblical history we have discussed in this chapter make it clear that we are in the end stages of the endtimes.

Just as there was war (brother against brother) at the Euphrates in the beginning, war will again emerge from the Euphrates region.

The only escape, I repeat, is Jesus Christ, who gives us the peace which passes all understanding!

CHAPTER THREE

Abraham, Our Father

Summary

Abraham is the father of the Hebrew people. This chapter examines his life of faith, which is set forth as an example for those of us who believe in Jesus Christ. Abraham is also called the father of all who believe. Furthermore, he is the father of the Arabs, too. We see how Abraham's faith, coupled with works of faith, attained the righteousness that counts before God.

T*he book of the generation of Jesus Christ, the Son of David, the son of Abraham"* (Matthew 1:1). Abraham is the patriarch of the Jewish people, and through him, the Jews have been elected by God as a special chosen nation. However, to isolate Abraham as the father of the Jews does not fulfill the extended promise God gave to this man personally. Therefore, we want to look into this matter and learn about the three groups of people on Earth today: Gentiles, Jews, and Christians.

These three groups are very distinct, but all three are directly connected to Father Abraham.

Abraham's Origin

Abraham's calling did not take place in the Promised Land, but in Ur of the Chaldees, in the land of Mesopotamia, not far from the geographic location of the Tower of Babel. According to Acts 7:2, *"...The God of glory appeared unto our father Abraham, when he was in Mesopotamia, before he dwelt in Charran."*

This land was the area of the Euphrates River where "paradise," or the Garden of Eden and Babylon, was also situated. Therefore, we must first deal with this greatly significant territory before moving on to discuss Abraham's life. Babylon is often called "the cradle of humanity," and no doubt, that is at least partially true because when God created man in His own image, He placed him in the Garden of Eden, located in that geographic area.

Thus, we have God's glory on Earth in paradise; we have the fall of man in paradise; and later the first murder—when Cain slew Abel—in paradise.

Before Abraham's calling, however, we find the description of the building of the Tower of Babel in Genesis 11 and the first attempt to create a united world order: *"And the whole earth was of one language, and of one speech.*

"And it came to pass, as they journeyed from the east, that they found a plain in the land of Shinar; and they dwelt there.

"And they said one to another, Go to, let us make brick, and burn them thoroughly. And they had brick for stone, and slime had they for morter.

"And they said, Go to, let us build us a city and a tower, whose top may reach unto heaven; and let us make us a name, lest we be scattered abroad upon the face of the whole earth" (Genesis 11:1–4).

Some have suggested that the building of the Tower of Babel was really a temple used for sacrifice to idols. Since we do not know, and the Tower of Babel was demolished long ago, we'll simply accept the Bible's description of a people who wanted world unity, fame, and obviously, a united religion. It's not surprising, therefore, that the last world empire carries the name of "Mystery Babylon," which derives from Babel. More on that subject later.

One Language
How did God react to this development? We have the answer in Genesis 11:6–7, *"And the LORD said, Behold, the people is one, and they have all one language; and this they begin to do: and now nothing will be restrained from them, which they have imagined to do.*

"Go to, let us go down, and there confound their language, that they may not understand one another's speech."

The result of God's judgment was that the people became incapable of fulfilling the imagination of their hearts, due to the confusion of languages.

The "Direction" of Salvation
The Tower of Babel also shows that man cannot please God or attain salvation by trying to reach from Earth to heaven.

But, in the reverse direction, God sent His Son from heaven to Earth and reconciled the world unto Himself!

Abraham Moves Out

Immediately after the judgment at the Tower of Babel, we read about a man called Abraham, *"And Terah took Abram his son, and Lot the son of Haran his son's son, and Sarai his daughter in law, his son Abram's wife; and they went forth with them from Ur of the Chaldees, to go into the land of Canaan; and they came unto Haran, and dwelt there.*

"And the days of Terah were two hundred and five years: and Terah died in Haran" (Genesis 11:31–32).

Abraham's father gathered the family, not Abraham alone as instructed. One son, Nahor, Abraham's brother, apparently stayed behind.

Abraham had very strong family ties. The commandment he had received from the Lord was apparently also applied to his father, and Lot, the son of Abraham's brother, Haran, who had died.

But, the Lord's message was plain, *"Now the LORD had said unto Abram, Get thee out of thy country, and from thy kindred, and from thy father's house, unto a land that I will shew thee"* (Genesis 12:1). Abraham was to divide himself from his country, his kindred, and from his father's house.

He was supposed to go with his wife alone, without carrying along father Terah and nephew Lot.

The attempt to emigrate to Canaan did not materialize at that time, because old father Terah stayed in Haran where he later died.

Here, we see the need for total surrender, which includes family and country. The Lord taught us, *"If any man come to me, and hate not his father, and mother, and wife, and children, and brethren, and sisters, yea, and his own life also, he cannot be my disciple"* (Luke 14:26).

What we learn from Abraham's life is that God does not intend to bring forth salvation through the unity of people, such as those who built the Tower of Babel.

Neither did He intend to move the entire family of Abraham to the Promised Land. The Lord worked through *segregation*, not integration.

He needed only one person to whom He could entrust His plan of salvation, which was built upon faith.

Unconditional Covenant

Adam and Eve believed what the deceiver told them, but Abraham believed God. With Abraham, therefore, God began to reveal His plan of salvation for mankind.

The blessing we read in Genesis 12:2–3 is still valid, *"And I will make of thee a great nation, and I will bless thee, and make thy name great; and thou shalt be a blessing:*

"And I will bless them that bless thee, and curse him that curseth thee: and in thee shall all families of the earth be blessed."

In the above passage, please note the three-fold "I will" of God:

1) He will make a great nation of Abraham.

2) It is the Lord that will bless him.

3) In Abraham, all the nations, all the families of the Earth, will be blessed.

These eternal principles have never been cancelled. Over the millennia, many nations and rulers have learned to understand this fact the hard way.

Abraham's nation, Israel, is again becoming great. In the end, all nations and families will be blessed through them!

Right here in the very beginning, we see Abraham's connection to the Gentiles; and for all practical purposes, he too was a Gentile.

But in this promise God gave to him personally, the distinction was made between his great nation, Israel, and the Gentile world, but making the blessing available to "all families of the Earth."

Lot Went With Him

After Abraham's father, Terah, had died, Abraham was ready to go to the land of Canaan. We read in Genesis 12:4, *"So Abram departed, as the LORD had spoken unto him; and Lot went with him: and Abram was seventy and five years old when he departed out of Haran."*

Why did Lot go along? Did Abraham just take him? The Bible does not give us an answer, but we may speculate that Abraham, at that time 75 years of age, having no children, might have thought that Lot, being his brother's son, would bring forth descendants.

Although we don't know why Lot went with him, one thing is clear: it was contradictory to the command God gave Abraham to leave his country, his relatives, and his father's house. If he would have left all, Lot could not come along.

Problem With Lot

It wasn't long before this companionship went sour. Genesis 13, verses 6 and 7, describe the situation: *"And the land was not able to bear them, that they might dwell together: for their substance was great, so that they could not dwell together.*

"And there was a strife between the herdmen of Abram's cattle and the herdmen of Lot's cattle: and the Canaanite and the Perizzite dwelled then in the land."

Interestingly enough, we don't see Lot separating himself from Uncle Abraham, which would have been normal, because Abraham was the one who had received the calling and he was the elder.

Although God had given His promise to Abraham and not to Lot, Abraham acted in a very generous manner, *"And Abram said unto Lot, Let there be no strife, I pray thee, between me and thee, and between my herdmen and thy herdmen; for we be brethren.*

"Is not the whole land before thee? separate thyself, I pray thee, from me: if thou wilt take the left hand, then I will go to the right; or if thou depart to the right hand, then I will go to the left" (Genesis 13:8–9).

Lot, acting selfishly, took advantage of Abraham's generosity, *"And Lot lifted up his eyes, and beheld all the plain of Jordan, that it was well watered every where, before the LORD destroyed Sodom and Gomorrah, even as the garden of the LORD, like the land of Egypt, as thou comest unto Zoar"* (Genesis 13:10).

Lot didn't receive the promise; thus, he relied not on the Lord, but on that which he saw: *"...Lot lifted up his eyes...."* The tragedy of Lot began here. He built his future on what he saw. However, the Bible says, *"But the men of Sodom were wicked and sinners before the LORD exceedingly"* (Genesis 13:13). Lot made a quintessential short-sighted decision based on worldly values. Later, we see what happened as a result of his toleration of the abominations of Sodom and Gomorrah.

Abraham's Holy Land Tour

To offset the loss and separation from Lot and his people, God instructed Abraham to undertake a Holy Land tour, *"And the LORD said unto Abram, after that Lot was separated from him, Lift up now thine eyes, and look from the*

*place where thou art northward, and southward, and east-
ward, and westward:*

*"For all the land which thou seest, to thee will I give it,
and to thy seed for ever.*

*"And I will make thy seed as the dust of the earth: so that
if a man can number the dust of the earth, then shall thy seed
also be numbered.*

*"Arise, walk through the land in the length of it and in the
breadth of it; for I will give it unto thee"* (Genesis
13:14–17).

Abraham was in contact with Almighty God, the Creator
of heaven and Earth. He received the promise that his seed
would inherit the land forever!

Lost Lot

But, nothing is written about Lot's walk with the Lord and
it wasn't long until he got into big trouble.

That which he chose, the plain of Jordan, where the cities
of Sodom and Gomorrah were located, came under attack
and all that he had was taken away: *"And they took Lot,
Abram's brother's son, who dwelt in Sodom, and his goods,
and departed"* (Genesis 14:12).

Not only did Lot lose all his earthly possessions, but now
he was taken prisoner and could expect to be sold as a slave
to the enemies.

The news reached Abraham, and without much thought,
he did everything in his power to free his nephew Lot. *"And
when Abram heard that his brother was taken captive, he
armed his trained servants, born in his own house, three
hundred and eighteen, and pursued them unto Dan.*

*"And he divided himself against them, he and his ser-
vants, by night, and smote them, and pursued them unto
Hobah, which is on the left hand of Damascus"* (Genesis
14:14–15).

The result is reported for us in verse 16, *"And he brought back all the goods, and also brought again his brother Lot, and his goods, and the women also, and the people."*

The King of Sodom

Abraham was rich, and now he was a military hero as well. He was also in the land of Canaan, promised to him by God.

As he returned victoriously from the mission to rescue Lot and his entourage, *"...the king of Sodom went out to meet him...."*

What did the king want? *"...Give me the persons and take the goods to thyself"* (verse 21). Here, we see a compromise being offered.

But Abraham, the spiritual man who believed in the living God, answered, *"...I have lift up mine hand unto the LORD, the most high God, the possessor of heaven and earth,*

"That I will not take from a thread even to a shoelatchet, and that I will not take any thing that is thine, lest thou shouldest say, I have made Abram rich" (Genesis 14:22–23).

Abraham's motive was clear: He did not desire to add to his riches, as apparently the king of Sodom imagined. Abraham only wanted to rescue his nephew Lot, which he did successfully.

Very firmly, he denied any relationship with Sodom. Clearly, we recognize the deception of the worldly blessing that was offered by the king of Sodom, which typifies the work of the Devil!

Melchizedek, King of Salem

Then, we read about a mysterious figure by the name of Melchizedek, whose name means "king of righteousness." *"And Melchizedek king of Salem brought forth bread and wine: and he was the priest of the most high God"* (Genesis 14:18).

While the bread and wine would have been refreshing to the exhausted soldiers of Abraham's army, I believe that these two items are prophetically pointing to the Lord Jesus Christ. This mysterious person was a king and also *"...the priest of the most high God."* He presented Abraham bread and wine.

We are reminded of our Lord Jesus, who *"...took bread: And when he had given thanks, he brake it, and said, Take, eat: this is my body, which is broken for you: this do in remembrance of me"* (1st Corinthians 11:23–24) Then the substance of the wine, *"After the same manner also he took the cup, when he had supped, saying, This cup is the new testament in my blood: this do ye, as oft as ye drink it, in remembrance of me"* (verse 25).

Abraham had spiritual discernment, the ability to distinguish the real from the fake.

He said "No" to the king of Sodom, but "Yes" to Melchizedek, king of Salem.

From this point of view, we understand Jesus' meaning when He said, *"Your father Abraham rejoiced to see my day: and he saw it, and was glad"* (John 8:56).

This meeting with Abraham was a prophetic demonstration of that which was to come. Melchizedek was compared with the Son of God, *"Without father, without mother, without descent, having neither beginning of days, nor end of life; but made like unto the Son of God; abideth a priest continually"* (Hebrews 7:3). I make the proposition that Melchizedek is not the Son of God because it very specifically says, *"...like unto the Son of God...."*

But, at the same time, the descriptions of Melchizedek in this passage, "without father...mother...descent...no beginning nor end, [etc.]" all have Messianic implications.

No doubt, this Scripture has tried the minds of Bible scholars for millennia.

Abraham Learns Patience

God led Abraham step-by-step, and in chapter 15, reconfirmed His promise He had given. But, then Abraham answered, *"...Lord GOD, what wilt thou give me, seeing I go childless...?"* (Genesis 15:2). Here, we see Abraham coming to the end of his faith. However, he did the right thing: he confessed it to God, and, as an answer, the Lord asked him to step outside. *"...Look now toward heaven, and tell the stars, if thou be able to number them: and he said unto him, So shall thy seed be"* (Genesis 15:5).

The next verse is of great significance: *"...he* [Abraham] *believed in the LORD; and he counted it to him for righteousness"* (verse 6). Abraham believed, although he saw no proof, and, we must add, was getting older day-by-day. So was his wife! Nevertheless, he believed!

Then, the Lord requests a sacrifice, *"...Take me an heifer of three years old, and a she goat of three years old, and a ram of three years old, and a turtledove, and a young pigeon"* (Genesis 15:9).

Afterward, God showed Abraham why he could not take possession of the Promised Land at that time, *"...Know of a surety that thy seed shall be a stranger in a land that is not theirs, and shall serve them; and they shall afflict them four hundred years.*

"But in the fourth generation they shall come hither again: for the iniquity of the Amorites is not yet full" (Verses 13 and 16). Why couldn't Abraham take possession of the land? Answer: *"...the iniquity of the Amorites is not yet full."* The grace of God was breaking through for the Amorites. Four-hundred years were given to them to repent or to add to their iniquity to the full.

This message is a two-edged sword: The Amorites received 400 years of *grace*, and Abraham's descendants, the Israelites, would have to *suffer* 400 years!

Abraham was being led closer and closer to God, relying more and more on Him, and in Genesis 15:18 we read, *"...Unto thy seed have I given this land, from the river of Egypt unto the great river, the river Euphrates."*

This promise no longer concerned the future, but in faith, it was already an accomplished fact: God had already given this land to Abraham's descendants!

Sarai's Unbelief

It seems that the enemy, which could not shake Abraham's faith, now aimed at his wife, Sarai. Apparently in vain, Abraham and Sarai waited for the long-promised son. One day, Sarai got an idea, *"...Behold now, the LORD hath restrained me from bearing: I pray thee, go in unto my maid; it may be that I may obtain children by her. And Abram hearkened to the voice of Sarai"* (Genesis 16:2).

That was the beginning of the Ishmaelites, predominately Egyptians. This self-help was not originally ordained, but later confirmed by God.

The promise to Hagar, the Egyptian, reads, *"And the angel of the LORD said unto her, I will multiply thy seed exceedingly, that it shall not be numbered for multitude"* (Genesis 16:10). The blessing was pronounced upon the Arabs even before Ishmael was born, *"...I will multiply thy seed exceedingly...."*

And then in verse 15 we read, *"And Hagar bare Abram a son: and Abram called his son's name, which Hagar bare, Ishmael."* Upon the birth of Ishmael, Abraham was 86 years old. For 14 years, Abraham waited and nothing happened. Ishmael appeared to be the heir of all that Abraham had, including the promises.

Promise At Age 99

But then, when Abraham was 99, God spoke to him, *"As for me, behold, my covenant is with thee, and thou shalt be a father of many nations.*

"Neither shall thy name any more be called Abram, but thy name shall be Abraham; for a father of many nations have I made thee" (Genesis 17:4–5). God acted in a different way than Abraham expected.

We, as believers, do well to realize that our thoughts and ways are not the thoughts and ways of God. You may be experiencing great difficulties, sickness, and loneliness. It may seem as if God does not care, but that's not the case.

He not only knows your situation very intimately, He knows all your thoughts ahead of time. He is the *"...discerner of the thoughts and intents of the heart"* (Hebrews 4:12).

He permits you to go through the valley of tribulation so you will cling to Him even more. He is your only hope. Never must you dishonor Him with the thought that He has forsaken you, because He promised, *"...lo, I am with you alway, even unto the end of the world"* (Matthew 28:20).

Abram Becomes Abraham

At the age of almost 100, Abraham's name was changed from Abram, meaning the "high or exalted father," to Abraham, which is translated "father of a great multitude" or "father of many nations."

Then, Abraham heard the promise God gave him, *"And I will make thee exceeding fruitful, and I will make nations of thee, and kings shall come out of thee.*

"And I will establish my covenant between me and thee and thy seed after thee in their generations for an everlasting covenant, to be a God unto thee, and to thy seed after thee.

"And I will give unto thee, and to thy seed after thee, the land wherein thou art a stranger, all the land of Canaan, for an everlasting possession; and I will be their God" (Genesis 17:6–8).

With the change of his name from Abram to Abraham, he received a detailed promise sealed with the words, *"...an everlasting covenant...."* And regarding the land, *"...an everlasting possession...."*

Sarai also received a change of name, *"...As for Sarai thy wife, thou shalt not call her name Sarai, but Sarah shall her name be.*

"And I will bless her, and give thee a son also of her: yea, I will bless her, and she shall be a mother of nations; kings of people shall be of her" (Genesis 17:15–16).

Prayer for Ishmael

This was just too much for Abraham to grasp. He thought that God had confirmed his son Ishmael, and began to pray, *"...O that Ishmael might live before thee!"* (verse 18). Quickly, God corrected him, *"Sarah thy wife shall bear thee a son indeed; and thou shalt call his name Isaac: and I will establish my covenant with him for an everlasting covenant, and with his seed after him"* (verse 19).

Even before Isaac was born, the distinction between Isaac and Ishmael was reconfirmed by God. The everlasting covenant was not to be established through Ishmael, but through Isaac.

Nevertheless, Ishmael was not forgotten, *"And as for Ishmael, I have heard thee: Behold, I have blessed him, and will make him fruitful, and will multiply him exceedingly; twelve princes shall he beget, and I will make him a great nation"* (Genesis 17:20). This passage is foundational concerning Abraham's connection to the Arab world: twelve princes and "a great nation."

Until this very day, Israel has noticed, often painfully, the "great nation" of the Arab world. They are indeed much greater in numbers, riches, and territory than Israel, which today is just a tiny spot in the Middle East. Israel is surrounded by gigantic Arab countries determined to destroy her.

Sodom and Gomorrah

In chapter 18, we again read of the reconfirmation of the birth of the promised son, Isaac.

But the reason for the appearance of the Lord to Abraham concerned another urgent matter: the city of Sodom where Lot resided. The judgment upon this city was of great significance. The Lord revealed the reason to Abraham, *"...Because the cry of Sodom and Gomorrah is great, and because their sin is very grievous;*

"I will go down now, and see whether they have done altogether according to the cry of it, which is come unto me; and if not, I will know" (Genesis 18:20–21).

Destruction of Sodom meant the end of Lot, too. Therefore, Abraham stood before the Lord and asked for mercy. He knew that his nephew Lot and all that he possessed was in the city.

Abraham presumed that there were 50 righteous people in that city and asked, *"...wilt thou also destroy and not spare the place for the fifty righteous that are therein?"* (verse 24). Abraham kept decreasing the number until he hoped that 10 righteous persons were in the city. The Lord answered, *"...I will not destroy it for ten's sake"* (Genesis 18:32).

What a wonderful man Abraham was. He could have said, in effect, "It was Lot's own fault to go to that place. He argued with my people. I gave him first choice. He selected the place. He got himself into this situation. I have done everything I could. Now let the Lord do what is right." That would have been the natural way of the flesh, but Abraham knew what it meant to have a priestly attitude. He was concerned for the souls of nephew Lot and his family!

Judgment Upon Sodom

Chapter 19 of Genesis describes the shocking confrontation between Lot and the citizens of the city who openly practiced homosexuality.

But, nowhere in the Scripture do we read that Lot fought against the Sodomites, actively protesting or campaigning to eradicate their sin.

In the New Testament, however, the Apostle Peter said this about Lot: *"And delivered just Lot, vexed with the filthy conversation of the wicked"* (2nd Peter 2:7). When reading the scriptural account about Lot's life, though, I can only see him as a terrible failure. When the angels of the Lord came to rescue him, he was challenged by the Sodomites; and instead of standing his ground, he went so far as to offer his two daughters to those wicked people! When he tried to warn his sons-in-law, the Bible says, *"...But he seemed as one that mocked unto his sons in law"* (Genesis 19:14). Lot obviously lacked backbone and character.

When the angels urged him, *"...he lingered...."* When the angels warned him, *"...Escape for thy life..."* he answered, *"...Oh, not so, my LORD."* Finally, he disgraced himself by committing incest. Nevertheless, Lot believed in the God of Abraham, and therefore, he was counted as one of the righteous.

We see the grace of God overwhelmingly demonstrated in Genesis 19:22, *"Haste thee, escape thither; for I cannot do any thing till thou be come thither...."*

What a gracious God! His determined judgment was delayed because of *one* righteous person!

This is, incidentally, a good picture of the absolute necessity for the Church of Jesus Christ to be removed before destructive judgment comes upon Earth. God will not allow His wrath to come upon Earth as long as the church is present. The entire Lot episode is overshadowed by faithful Abraham. Genesis 19:29 reads, *"And it came to pass, when God destroyed the cities of the plain, that God remembered Abraham, and sent Lot out of the midst of the overthrow, when he overthrew the cities in the which Lot dwelt"* (Genesis 19).

Abraham's Test of Faith

Abraham's priestly attitude and immediate obedience to the Word of God brought him to the place where God could show His intention to save mankind:

"And it came to pass after these things, that God did tempt Abraham, and said unto him, Abraham: and he said, Behold, here I am.

"And he said, Take now thy son, thine only son Isaac, whom thou lovest, and get thee into the land of Moriah; and offer him there for a burnt offering upon one of the mountains which I will tell thee of" (Genesis 22:1–2).

This must have been a great shock to Abraham. He had waited so long for the promised son, praying for 25 years, and finally when he could see his beloved son, talk to him and enjoy the child, God said, *"...Take now thy son, thine only son Isaac, whom thou lovest, and get thee into the land of Moriah; and offer him there for a burnt offering...."*

Note that God says, *"...thine only son...."* As far as the promise was concerned, Ishmael was not included; only Isaac, the son *"whom thou lovest"* was chosen. We are reminded of John 3:16, *"For God so loved the world, that he gave his only begotten Son, that whosoever believeth in him should not perish, but have everlasting life."*

Under normal circumstances, Abraham should have called his wife Sarah immediately. They should have prayed about the matter. The elders of his little empire should have arranged a meeting to decide what to do in the great hour of need.

Surely, it must have been a mistake. Abraham was an old man, and he probably misunderstood. A prayer meeting should have been called and all would have diligently sought the countenance of the Lord to get an answer to this terrible dilemma.

They could have said, "Under no circumstances should Isaac die, for he is the promised son, and Abraham and Sarah are old people." However, Hebrews 11:11 testifies, *"Through faith also Sara herself received strength to conceive seed, and was delivered of a child when she was past age, because she judged him faithful who had promised."* She was too old to bear children!

Abraham Acts In Faith

How did Abraham react? Verse 3: *"And Abraham rose up early in the morning...."* There was no prayer, no discussion, no doubt, but immediate obedience to the commandment of the Lord.

He had to travel a long way, and on the third day, he saw Mount Moriah afar off.

Isaac, the only beloved son, is a picture of the Lord Jesus Christ, who obediently did all things the Father commanded. Just as the Lord Jesus carried His own cross, Isaac carried the wood for the burnt offering upon which he would be sacrificed!

Faith Sees A Substitute

Then, the moment came when Abraham demonstrated his obedience, unconditionally willing to sacrifice his son. But, then at the very last moment, *"...the angel of the LORD called unto him out of heaven, and said, Abraham, Abraham: and he said, Here am I.*

"And he said, Lay not thine hand upon the lad, neither do thou any thing unto him: for now I know that thou fearest God, seeing thou hast not withheld thy son, thine only son from me" (Genesis 22:11–12).

The reason Abraham followed God's command is reported in Hebrews 11:17–19, *"By faith Abraham, when he was tried, offered up Isaac: and he that had received the promises offered up his only begotten son,*

"Of whom it was said, That in Isaac shall thy seed be called:

"Accounting that God was able to raise him up, even from the dead; from whence also he received him in a figure."

That is faith which pleases God!

Genesis then reports that Abraham found a substitute, *"And Abraham lifted up his eyes, and looked, and behold behind him a ram caught in a thicket by his horns: and Abraham went and took the ram, and offered him up for a burnt offering in the stead of his son"* (Genesis 22:13).

Oh, how glad I am that a substitute was found, who died in my place, for my sin, and provided eternal salvation!

Abraham: The Father of the Arabs

We have already seen that Abraham's son Ishmael received the promise of being a great nation. This has been fulfilled, especially in recent years, because of the virtual Arab monopoly of the oil from below.

Ishmael, however, is not the only son of Abraham who can be considered Arab. There is an additional report of more of Abraham's children. *"Then again Abraham took a wife, and her name was Keturah.*

"And she bare him Zimran, and Jokshan, and Medan, and Midian, and Ishbak, and Shuah" (Genesis 25:1–2).

A closer name search reveals that these six sons of Abraham by Keturah are to be found in the Arab world. Midian, for example, became a fierce enemy of Israel. Jokshan's sons, Sheba and Dedan, are mentioned in Ezekiel 38 as being part of the Israeli neighbors who protest against the northern confederate invasion of the land of Israel, asking three protesting questions:

1) *"...Art thou come to take a spoil?..."*
2) *"...Has thou gathered thy company to take a prey?..."*
3) *"...To carry away silver and gold, to take away cattle and goods to take a great spoil?"* (Ezekiel 38:13).

The doomed great invasion of Gog and Magog, with their allies, Persia, Ethiopia, Libya, Gomer and Togarmah, is yet to take place. When it does, the surrounding Arab countries will naturally ask the protesting questions because they will realize that they, too, are at risk.

Already in our day, we are seeing growing diplomatic relations between Togarmah (Turkey) and their southeastern neighbor, Persia (Iran). The religion of the Arabs, which is based on the Qur'an, also claims Abraham as the father of the Arabs. Of course, it does not correspond to our Bible, for the Muslims believe that Abraham sacrificed Ishmael instead of Isaac.

Abraham, Father of the Jews

The fact that the Jews are the chosen biological descendants of Abraham does not need additional documentation. The Bible makes it clear that God's promise was passed on to Abraham's son Isaac, *"Sojourn in this land, and I will be with thee, and will bless thee; for unto thee, and unto thy* seed, I will give all these countries, and I will perform the oath which I sware unto Abraham thy father;

"And I will make thy seed to multiply as the stars of heaven, and will give unto thy seed all these countries; and in thy seed shall all the nations of the earth be blessed" (Genesis 26:3–4).

That same promise was given to Jacob, "And thy seed shall be as the dust of the earth, and thou shalt spread abroad to the west, and to the east, and to the north, and to the south: and in thee and in thy seed shall all the families of the earth be blessed" (Genesis 28:14).

Moses reinforces the promise to the children of Israel, "The secret things belong unto the LORD our God: but those things which are revealed belong unto us and to our children for ever, that we may do all the words of this law" (Deuteronomy 29:29). Later in history, we hear the Prophet Isaiah proclaim the Lord's message to Israel, which includes the restoration of the Promised Land, based on the blessing of Abraham, "Look unto Abraham your father, and unto Sarah that bare you: for I called him alone, and blessed him, and increased him.

"For the LORD shall comfort Zion: he will comfort all her waste places; and he will make her wilderness like Eden, and her desert like the garden of the LORD; joy and gladness shall be found therein, thanksgiving, and the voice of melody" (Isaiah 51:2–3).

Upon the birth of John the Baptist, his father Zechariah referred to this promise, "To perform the mercy promised to our fathers, and to remember his holy covenant;

"The oath which he sware to our father Abraham" (Luke 1:72–73). And the Lord Jesus confirmed in Matthew 3:9 that the Jews are the chosen people, but He prophetically added those who will also receive the promise of Abraham, "And think not to say within yourselves, We have Abraham *to our father: for I say unto you, that God is able of these stones to raise up children unto Abraham."*

Abraham, Father of Christians

Biologically speaking, the gentiles are aliens from the covenant of Israel, living without God and having no hope. But through *"...Jesus Christ, the son of David, the son of Abraham,"* we have become partakers of the blessing of Abraham. The Apostle Paul makes this obvious in Galatians 3:6–9, *"Even as Abraham believed God, and it was accounted to him for righteousness.*

"Know ye therefore that they which are of faith, the same are the children of Abraham.

"And the scripture, foreseeing that God would justify the heathen through faith, preached before the gospel unto Abraham, saying, In thee shall all nations be blessed.

"So then they which be of faith are blessed with faithful Abraham."

Through faith in Jesus Christ, the Son of God, we are integrated into the family of Abraham's faith, *"That the blessing of Abraham might come on the Gentiles through Jesus Christ; that we might receive the promise of the Spirit through faith"* (Galatians 3:14).

This last group of people, the Church of Jesus Christ, does not consist exclusively of Gentiles, but of Jews as well.

Verse 28 of Galatians 3 has this to say, *"There is neither Jew nor Greek, there is neither bond nor free, there is neither male nor female: for ye are all one in Christ Jesus."* This new nation of people scattered around the globe is one body in the Lord Jesus Christ. This verse is strictly concerned with a spiritual matter. It is important to point out that it does not support the ecumenical movement by which the various denominations join into one, even including other religions.

While spiritually we are one, this verse demonstrates the physical diversity between Jew and Greek, bond and free, male and female. Each one of us, born-again of the Spirit of God, remains the same as we were before in our biological, physical body: A male remains a male, a female remains female. But in spirit, we have become Abraham's seed, *"And if ye be Christ's, then are ye Abraham's seed, and heirs according to the promise"* (Galatians 3:29).

Works or Faith?
With this, we come to our last question which needs to be emphasized: "Is salvation obtained by works or by faith?" Often we hear religious people quote James 2:24, *"Ye see then how that by works a man is justified, and not by faith only."*

In seeming contrast, we read in Galatians 2:16, *"Knowing that a man is not justified by the works of the law, but by the faith of Jesus Christ, even we have believed in Jesus Christ, that we might be justified by the faith of Christ, and not by the works of the law: for by the works of the law shall no flesh be justified."*

Why does it seem that James is contradicting the clear teaching that, by faith alone, we can be saved? Romans 4:9 emphasizes, *"...faith was reckoned to Abraham for righteousness."*

I believe we have the answer in Hebrews 11:17, *"By faith Abraham, when he was tried, offered up Isaac: and he that had received the promises offered up his only begotten son."* This *work* was an act of *faith*. If Abraham would not have had the *faith*, he would not have produced the *work*.

True faith produces works of faith, but faith without works is in reality not the faith that saves, but simply a counterfeit faith which is not anchored in the Lord Jesus Christ. James says, *"Thou believest that there is one God; thou doest well: the devils also believe, and tremble"* (James 2:19). Thus, my question to you is, "Do you have faith in Jesus Christ?" The Bible says, *"...whosoever believeth in him should not perish, but have eternal life"* (John 3:15).

The clear distinction between those who believe in Jesus and others who do not is described in verse 36, *"He that believeth on the Son hath everlasting life: and he that believeth not the Son shall not see life; but the wrath of God abideth on him"* (John 3). Therefore, today, make sure that your faith is a living faith in the Lord Jesus Christ, which produces works that create fruit for eternity to His glory!

CHAPTER FOUR

Rebuilding The Second Temple

Summary

This chapter presents a prophetic analysis of Israel's rebuilding of the Temple in Jerusalem after returning from a 70-year captivity in Babylon. We show how the pagan King Cyrus of Persia followed God's instruction, and how Israel failed, at the beginning, to do God's bidding. This story also typifies the Church of Jesus Christ in the end-times.

After Babylon had fallen, we see that the God of Israel used a leader of another empire, Cyrus, King of Persia to fulfill His plan. *"Now in the first year of Cyrus king of Persia, that the word of the LORD by the mouth of Jeremiah might be fulfilled, the LORD stirred up the spirit of Cyrus king of Persia, that he made a proclamation throughout all his kingdom, and put it also in writing, saying,*

"Thus saith Cyrus king of Persia, The LORD God of heaven hath given me all the kingdoms of the earth; and he hath charged me to build him an house at Jerusalem, which is in Judah.

"And whosoever remaineth in any place where he sojourneth, let the men of his place help him with silver, and with gold, and with goods, and with beasts, beside the freewill offering for the house of God that is in Jerusalem" (Ezra 1:3). King Cyrus recognized the God of Israel as the true God. He made it his task to support the Jewish people to return to their land and rebuild the Temple which the king of Babylon had destroyed. The pagan king of Persia did that which was pleasing unto the Lord, but Israel did not, as we will see in a moment.

The City is Built
It is fascinating to read the Book of Ezra and discover how Israel misplaced their priorities regarding the clear instruction they had received. The commandment was very plain: *"Build the house of the Lord God of Israel...which is in Jerusalem."*

When the Jews returned with much riches, political authority, and the positive commandment of King Cyrus, they didn't go about rebuilding the Temple. It took the enemies of Israel to reveal the truth about the work of the Jews and expose them to the king of Persia. In a letter, they clearly identified the work they were doing; *"...building the rebellious and the bad city..."* (Ezra 4:12).

Repeatedly, the letter stated that the Jews were building the *city*. Nothing was said about the Temple.

The enemies made a justifiable accusation against the Jews, *"Be it known unto the king, that the Jews which came up from thee to us are come unto Jerusalem, building the rebellious and the bad city, and have set up the walls thereof, and joined the foundations...*

"We certify the king that, if this city be builded again, and the walls thereof set up, by this means thou shalt have no portion on this side the river" (Ezra 4:12,16).

What was the king's answer?

"Give ye now commandment to cause these men to cease, and that this city be not builded, until another commandment shall be given from me" (Ezra 4:21).

Then we read of a great tragedy in verse 24, *"Then ceased the work of the house of God which is at Jerusalem...."*

Another Warning to Us

What a tremendous lesson for the church! We must do that which we are commanded to do. All other things are secondary. The moment we fail to do our task, we will be forced, often unknowingly, to do something else, which ends up being the *Devil's* bidding!

No matter how important "something else" is, how noble a task it may be, or how urgent it is, it will never stand before God who gave us a clear commandment, *"Go ye into all the world, and preach the gospel to every creature"* (Mark 16:15).

Houses First, Temple Second

During the time that Israel was rebuilding the Temple, they certainly had all the reasons in the world to rebuild the walls of Jerusalem for protection, to build houses so they could live like human beings, educate their children, and take care of their families. All of these things were valid arguments, but they forgot the prime reason for their return to Jerusalem: *"...build the house of the LORD God of Israel..."* (Ezra 1:3).

This is not my interpretation, but this is simple Bible truth. Haggai testifies that Israel failed to do God's bidding, that is, build the Temple. Instead, they took care of their personal needs first, *"...This people say, The time is not come, the time that the LORD'S house should be built.*

"Then came the word of the LORD by Haggai the prophet, saying,

"Is it time for you, O ye, to dwell in your cieled houses, and this house lie waste?

"...Why? saith the LORD of hosts. Because of mine house that is waste, and ye run every man unto his own house" (Haggai 1:2–4; 9).

This must have been a terrible time for the Jews in Jerusalem. They had returned from a 70-year captivity, and during those long years, they had heard much about Jerusalem, the glorious Temple, and the wonderful works of God among them.

No doubt, the old people told the young ones; it was passed on from parents to the children.

Judaism was practiced while in dispersion, and based on the Scripture, many greatly prospered. The Jewish heart was directed toward the return to Zion, the rebuilding of the glorious Temple and the presence of God among His people in their own land.

However, as we have seen in the above Scripture verses, they slightly deviated from the priority and got on the wrong track. Now they had their hands full with all kinds of problems and worries.

Why? Simply because they had not been obedient to the king's command, which the *Lord* had given. This entire confusion could have been avoided easily if only they had precisely and immediately performed what they had been sent to do. There was no excuse as to the financial support; the king had given it to them. Even security was not really an issue because the king offered protection for the Jews. Surely, they would have been hard-pressed if asked for a reason why they had not been busy immediately building the Temple of the Lord. They had it all, but wasted it when they reversed the priorities.

The Prophetic Word
Finally, we see two prophets, Haggai and Zechariah, stand up and do the right thing. When these two prophets spoke, we notice the words, *"...build this house of God...."*

How did this turn of events come about? Obviously, it began with their attention to the prophetic Word. Where did the prophetic Word originate?

With God who inspired Cyrus, the king of Persia, to give commandment to let the Jews return to Jerusalem, *"...build the house of the LORD God of Israel...."*

But, the Jews who had returned to Jerusalem for the purpose of rebuilding the Temple occupied themselves with the infrastructure of their own living quarters and security. Nevertheless, the commandment to build the house of the Lord was still valid.

These two prophets had received wisdom from God. They did not bother about the errors that had been made regarding the building of *"...the rebellious and bad city...."* Rather, they highlighted the command: *"Build this house of God!"*

Opposition and Victory

As soon as they started to build the Temple, there was immediate opposition. *"...Who hath commanded you to build this house, and to make up this wall?*

"Then said we unto them after this manner, What are the names of the men that make this building?" (Ezra 5:3–4).

This sounds like a government inquiry. It was serious business; no one dared to oppose the king's command. Now, everything depended upon the reply of the Jews and here we see the grace of God breaking through once again, *"But the eye of their God was upon the Jews..."* (verse 5).

The elders wrote a letter to the king detailing the entire history regarding the reason and the legal rights as to the building of the house of God.

When we read the rest of chapter 5, we notice that the elders of Israel no longer mentioned the city, but rather, the house of God, *"...and build the house that was builded these many years ago..."* (verse 11); *"...to build this house of God"* (verse 13); *"...let the house of God be builded..."* (verse 15); *"...the foundation of the house of God which is in Jerusalem..."* (verse 16).

Ezra 5:17 then concludes, *"Now therefore, if it seem good to the king, let there be search made in the king's treasure house, which is there at Babylon, whether it be so, that a decree was made of Cyrus the king to build this house of God at Jerusalem, and let the king send his pleasure to us concerning this matter."*

Our Lesson

If only we would learn from this event to do the will of God. How do we know His will? We have a contract: the Bible. There, the commandment is written to go into all the world and preach the Gospel to every creature. If we do that, all other things become secondary.

Jesus said, *"But seek ye first the kingdom of God, and his righteousness; and all these things shall be added unto you"* (Matthew 6:33). The moment we occupy ourselves with fulfilling the Lord's commandment, we will not have time, energy or finances for the political arena, which belongs to the prince of darkness, the god of the world.

This is not our world. I'm sorry to disappoint you, but the U.S.A., Canada, nor any other country is really ours. Why? Because we are just passing through on our way to eternal glory!

Taxes for the Temple

Let's read the answer to the letter the Jews sent to the king, *"Then Darius the king made a decree, and search was made in the house of the rolls, where the treasures were laid up in Babylon.*

"And there was found at Achmetha, in the palace that is in the province of the Medes, a roll, and therein was a record thus written:

"In the first year of Cyrus the king the same Cyrus the king made a decree concerning the house of God at Jerusalem, Let the house be builded..." (Ezra 6:1–3).

This statement, indeed, must have rejoiced the heart of Israel. But there is more, *"...let the expenses be given out of the king's house"* (verse 4). This project was financed by the king of the land of their captivity!

If only they would have continued building the house of God, the financial question would have been solved. They did not need to save or sell "church bonds," go to the bank to get a loan, or get promissory notes from the congregation. It all was paid by the king! Furthermore, verse 5 documents the restoration of the things that belong to the Temple, *"And also let the golden and silver vessels of the house of God, which Nebuchadnezzar took forth out of the temple which is at Jerusalem, and brought unto Babylon, be restored, and brought again unto the temple which is at Jerusalem, every one to his place, and place them in the house of God."*

Build "This House of God"

After having read the documentation, King Darius warned the governor in charge of the territory of Jerusalem, *"Let the work of this house of God alone; let the governor of the Jews and the elders of the Jews build this house of God in his place"* (verse 7). Notice the center of the entire message again, *"...this house of God...."* They were commanded not to hinder the interest of the Jews. The commandment continues, *"Moreover I make a decree what ye shall do to the elders of these Jews for the building of this house of God: that of the king's goods, even of the tribute beyond the river, forthwith expenses be given unto these men, that they be not hindered"* (verse 8).

Even the animals for sacrifice were taken care of, *"And that which they have need of, both young bullocks, and rams, and lambs, for the burnt offerings of the God of heaven, wheat, salt, wine, and oil, according to the appointment of the priests which are at Jerusalem, let it be given them day by day without fail: That they may offer sacrifices of sweet savours unto the God of heaven, and pray for the life of the king, and of his sons"* (Verses 9–10).

Prophecy Fulfilled

What was the result of obeying the prophetic Word? *"And the elders of the Jews builded, and they prospered through the prophesying of Haggai the prophet and Zechariah the son of Iddo. And they builded, and finished it, according to the commandment of the God of Israel, and according to the commandment of Cyrus, and Darius, and Artaxerxes king of Persia"* (Ezra 6:14).

These few examples teach us that believers are subject to the government which God installs. Romans 13 has always been valid, *"Let every soul be subject unto the higher powers. For there is no power but of God: the powers that be are ordained of God"* (Romans 13:1).

During Ezra's case, the commandment was given by a pagan king, addressed to God's chosen people. That seems contradictory, but the Scripture we have just read identifies that the commandment of Cyrus was *"the commandment of the God of Israel...."*

CHAPTER FIVE

Israel And Judah

Summary

This chapter reveals the distinctive difference between Judah and Israel, but
documents how, through Judah, all
twelve tribes became Jews yet retained
their combined identity as Israel.

no "lost" tribes! This is why they are called 'Jews'.

Having identified the beginning of the Babylonian spirit during the building of the Tower of Babel, let's take a closer look at the nation of Israel. No one speaks more about Babylon than does the Prophet Jeremiah.

The Lord called Jeremiah when Josiah, the son of Amon, was the king over Judah. In the first 19 chapters, the prophet concerned himself almost exclusively with his own people, the Jews.

Relentlessly, Jeremiah uncovered the sins of the people of Judah. He primarily targeted the priesthood and the prophets who prophesied for personal gain.

No doubt, it was a difficult time for the kingdom of Judah because Israel was led away captive and ceased to be an independent nation. Let's, therefore, take a closer look at Israel.

Who is Israel?

Although the nation of Israel as separate identity from Judah ceased to exist, Israel continued nevertheless, because Judah and Benjamin also belong to Israel.

Second Chronicles 11:14 and 16 makes the following statement, *"For the Levites left their suburbs and their possession, and came to Judah and Jerusalem: for Jeroboam and his sons had cast them off from executing the priest's office unto the Lord....*

"And after them out of all the tribes of Israel such as set their hearts to seek the Lord God of Israel came to Jerusalem, to sacrifice unto the Lord God of their fathers."

Second Chronicles 15:9 reinforces the integration of the so-called "ten lost tribes" into the tribe of Judah, *"And he gathered all Judah and Benjamin, and the strangers with them out of Ephraim and Manasseh, and out of Simeon: for they fell to him out of Israel in abundance, when they saw that the Lord his God was with him."*

These Scriptures should settle the issue regarding the ten lost tribes of Israel because there are no ten lost tribes. As we've just seen, they were integrated into the tribe of Judah—they became Jews.

The rest of the people of those ten tribes lost all legal rights to be part of God's chosen people, because they ceased to be part of Judah. While Judah was always part of Israel, Israel was never counted as part of Judah. To keep their identity, the ten separated tribes had to come to Judah.

As we've just read in the various Scripture quotations, a great number of those ten separated tribes joined themselves to the tribe of Judah and became Jews, but the rest didn't and, based on my understanding of the Scripture, they'll never be reattached to the identity of Judah's Israel.

Israel and Jews are Identical

The New Testament doesn't give us much information about the identity of the various tribes of Israel, but after the birth of Jesus, we read about a certain Anna, a prophetess, who was of the tribe of Asher.

Furthermore, the testimony of the Apostle Paul clearly stated, *"I also am an Israelite...of the tribe of Benjamin"* (Romans 11:1). I think that should further strengthen the legitimacy of why Jews call themselves Israelites.

These things are important to understand so we'll not be confused by those who teach that the ten lost tribes of Israel migrated to Europe, and therefore the European nations—particularly the "Anglo-Saxons"—are now the true descendants of Israel. The Bible exposes such teaching as false and no further discussion is needed.

We conclude that the names and descriptions, such as Jews, Israelites, and Hebrews, are applicable and interchangeable to all descendants of the twelve tribes of Israel who have established their identity in the tribe of Judah.

The Twelve Tribes

Now that we've seen the twelve tribes of Israel finding their identity in the tribe of Judah, the logical question comes to mind: "Have the names of the twelve tribes of Israel and their geographic inheritance been obliterated forever?" This is the case if we believe that all have been integrated into the tribe of Judah. Thus, we need to study this matter further.

In Genesis 49, we read about the twelve blessings upon Jacob's sons. This chapter starts off, *"And Jacob called unto his sons, and said, gather yourselves together, that I may tell you that which shall befall you in the last days"* (verse 1). The most detailed blessing is given to the eleventh son, Joseph. He was the lost son of Israel, but he became their savior. Also important to mention is the second longest blessing upon Judah, from which the Savior would come forth, *"The sceptre shall not depart from Judah, nor a law-giver from between his feet, until Shiloh come; and unto him shall the gathering of the people be"* (Genesis 49:10).

After Jacob had pronounced all the blessings and charged his sons regarding his burial, we read in verse 33, *"And when Jacob had made an end of commanding his sons, he gathered up his feet into the bed, and yielded up the ghost, and was gathered unto his people."* There's no proof in this chapter that some of the tribes would be obliterated. Therefore, we must conclude that Israel, all twelve tribes, will continue to exist.

Moses' Blessings

Later in history, Moses also pronounced a prophetic blessing upon the twelve tribes in Deuteronomy 33, *"And this is the blessing, wherewith Moses the man of God blessed the children of Israel before his death"* (verse 1).

He then ended the blessing with a summary for all the tribes, *"Happy art thou, O Israel: who is like unto thee, O people saved by the LORD, the shield of thy help, and who is the sword of thy excellency! and thine enemies shall be found liars unto thee; and thou shalt tread upon their high places"* (Deuteronomy 33:29).

New Testament and the Twelve Tribes

In the blessing of Moses, we see no proof that the twelve tribes and their identities would be done away with. Therefore, we believe that although the twelve tribes found their identity in the tribe of Judah and have become Jews today, God's choosing of the twelve tribes is eternal.

The existence of the twelve tribes is identified during New Testament times in James 1:1, *"James, a servant of God and of the Lord Jesus Christ, to the twelve tribes which are scattered abroad, greeting."*

And finally, in Revelation 21:12, we read, *"And the heavenly city had a wall great and high, and had twelve gates, and at the gates twelve angels, and names written thereon, which are the names of the twelve tribes of the children of Israel."* This documents the eternal existence of the twelve tribes of Israel. Furthermore, the existence of the twelve tribes of Israel within the Jews is also shown for us in Revelation 7:5–8, *"Of the tribe of Juda were sealed twelve thousand. Of the tribe of Reuben were sealed twelve thousand. Of the tribe of Gad were sealed twelve thousand.*

"Of the tribe of Aser were sealed twelve thousand. Of the tribe of Nepthalim were sealed twelve thousand. Of the tribe of Manasses were sealed twelve thousand.

"Of the tribe of Simeon were sealed twelve thousand. Of the tribe of Levi were sealed twelve thousand. Of the tribe of Issachar were sealed twelve thousand.

"Of the tribe of Zabulon were sealed twelve thousand. Of the tribe of Joseph were sealed twelve thousand. Of the tribe of Benjamin were sealed twelve thousand."

This chapter speaks of the time when the church is in the presence of the Lord, raptured, and the Great Tribulation has begun.

During that time, Israel will experience the most horrible suffering in its history because of the threat that its identity may be obliterated from the Earth.

The Future of the Twelve Tribes

We must understand that during the Tribulation, the whole world will be united. Finally, man will live at peace, in great prosperity, and only one government will rule the world, headed by the Antichrist. His success will be so great that, *"All that dwell upon the Earth shall worship him..."* (Revelation 13:8).

During that period, it will become evident that the Jews are different and they can't be fully integrated into the New World Order. Before God sends judgment upon the Earth, He gives a command, *"Saying, Hurt not the earth, neither the sea, nor the trees, till we have sealed the servants of our God in their foreheads.*

"And I heard the number of them which were sealed: and there were sealed an hundred and forty and four thousand of all the tribes of the children of Israel" (Revelation 7:3–4).

Again, we must stress that this relates to Israel, to the Jewish people. God will reveal the identity of each tribe, which today is hidden from the Jewish people. This should be enough to show the reality of the twelve tribes of Israel for now and eternity. Not only is the identity of Israel and the twelve tribes a Biblical reality, but the proper geographical division of the Promised Land will also happen.

In the prophetic vision of Ezekiel, we read, *"So shall ye divide this land unto you according to the tribes of Israel"* (Ezekiel 47:21).

Chapter 48 clearly documents the geographical division for the twelve tribes of the children of Israel.

Despite what the nations do or what the politicians say, the Word of God is eternally true and His prophecies will be fulfilled in their finest detail.

Ezekiel concludes, *"This is the land which ye shall divide by lot unto the tribes of Israel for inheritance, and these are their portions, saith the Lord GOD"* (Ezekiel 48:29).

Geographical Inheritance

The most visible problem in Israel today is territory. Most of the Promised Land is occupied by Arabs. Palestinian settlers are demanding that Jews surrender a large part of the Promised Land so they can form an additional Arab nation called "Palestine." This ridiculous request is being taken seriously by the whole world. No nation under God's sun dares to stand up and say "The land from the Euphrates River to the river of Egypt is the inheritance of the children of Israel and should become part of the Jewish state."

Such a statement would be politically impossible and most certainly would be laughable for the nations of the world. Also, few in Israel would dare to make such a proposition because the territory of the Promised Land is solidly divided and secured by so-called "internationally recognized borders." Not in their wildest dreams could anyone imagine that Syria would vacate the land up to the Euphrates River. Nor would the people of Lebanon return to the land of their forefathers somewhere outside the borders of the Promised Land. Neither would King Hussein surrender one inch of the territory he now holds.

So, in plain words, it's totally impossible for Israel to take ownership of the Promised Land within the borders outlined by God. The whole world agrees that Israel must not be allowed to expand her borders.

The question isn't how much territory Israel can take possession of. The opposite is true: The world is forcing Israel to surrender more of the Promised Land to Arab settlers. But this way of thinking—that it's impossible for Israel to take possession of the whole Promised Land—is dead wrong.

How Great Are the Superpowers?

We're overestimating, by far, the power and importance of the nations. What the president of the United States, the chairman of China, the president of Russia, the chancellor of Germany, or the prime minister of Britain thinks, says or does, may be extremely important to the world's population, but from God's perspective, these issues are less than nothing! Psalm 2 describes the commotion, protests and opposition of the rulers of this world, *"Why do the heathen rage, and the people imagine a vain thing?*

"The kings of the earth set themselves, and the rulers take counsel together, against the LORD, and against his anointed, saying,

"Let us break their bands asunder, and cast away their cords from us" (verses 1–3).

We have to admit that these "kings" and "rulers" have some mighty power at their disposal. Think of the armed forces, the nuclear weapons, the mighty industrial power-bases. We're told that a nuclear war could devastate the globe, obliterate every living soul and turn this planet into a smoking cinder, so we should admit that people have power over the Earth.

God Laughs At the Nations

But what's God's reaction? *"He that sitteth in the heavens shall laugh: the Lord shall have them in derision.*

"Then shall he speak unto them in his wrath, and vex them in his sore displeasure" (Verses 4–5). This verse has

refreshed me repeatedly: God laughs at the nations! As far as God is concerned, the pitiful little U.S.A., the U.N., China, Russia, and the New World Order are just a joke for our heavenly Father, the Creator of heaven and Earth! His answer isn't a united world, some imposing global society, the New World Order, or any nation that may be named on Earth.

What, then, is His answer? *"Yet have I set my king upon my holy hill of Zion"* (verse 6). The answer to the world's controversy will be Zion, which has been shown through Zionism, the driving force behind the reestablishment of the State of Israel.

The insignificance of the nations is furthermore emphasized in Isaiah 40:17, *"All nations before him are as nothing; and they are counted to him less than nothing, and vanity."*

It's my prayer that these few Scriptures show to us the insignificance of our nation or any other and the overwhelming importance of our Lord!

CHAPTER SIX

The Terror of Babylon

Summary

Identifying *Mystery Babylon* leads us to discover the amazing success of democracy. Contrary to the beliefs of many, Mystery Babylon will not come into power by force, but *"by peace* [he] *shall destroy many"*…*"he shall come in peaceably"*…*"*[he shall]…*obtain the kingdom by flatteries"*…*"He shall enter peaceably…"*

W e cannot read the Bible without confronting Babylon and its effects. In fact, the word "Babylon" appears 286 times in the Bible, with 12 of those instances appearing in the New Testament.

Unger's Bible Dictionary highlights the meaning under the word "Babylon":

> "An ancient city-state in the plain of Shinar, derived from Accadian bebilu ("gate of god").
>
> 1. Name. The name is derived by the Hebrews from the root balal ("to confound"), and has reference to the confusion of tongues at the Tower (Genesis 11:9). Thus the Biblical writer refutes any God-honoring connotation of the name. The Biblical account ascribes the founding of the ancient prehistoric city of Babylon to the descendants of Cush and the followers of Nimrod (Genesis 19:8–10). This statement distinguishes the people who founded the city (evidently the Sumerians) from the Semitic-Babylonians who afterward possessed it."

It is highly interesting that at the mention of the first Babylon (Babel), we see a form of democracy at work; an attempt to fully unite the world politically, economically and religiously.

Let's read the first four verses of Genesis 11: *"And the whole earth was of one language, and of one speech.*

"And it came to pass, as they journeyed from the east, that they found a plain in the land of Shinar; and they dwelt there.

"And they said one to another, Go to, let us make brick, and burn them thoroughly. And they had brick for stone, and slime had they for mortar.

"And they said, Go to, let us build us a city and a tower, whose top may reach unto heaven; and let us make us a

name, lest we be scattered abroad upon the face of the whole earth."

The center of civilization, therefore, was the city of Babel. Archaeologists today believe that the infamous tower was located somewhere close to the ancient city of Babylon in today's Iraq.

Democracy At Work

Let me highlight some important aspects of the building of the Tower of Babel. This great undertaking was not authorized by a powerful emperor, king, or great warrior. Instead, the people of the land were the driving force behind the undertaking. Specifically, verse 4 reinforces this, *"...they said...let us build us a city and a tower...."* We read of no opposition. The people were in charge of their own affairs. They apparently were united in their drive toward this ancient world society.

New Building Materials

Also noteworthy is the fact that to undertake such a gigantic project, the Babylonians could not rely on the building materials—stone and mortar—that were readily available to them: *"...they had brick for stone, and slime had they for mortar."* They had to unify the building materials by making bricks: *"...let us make brick, and burn them thoroughly...."*

The ingredients for mortar are plentifully available all over the world. Basically, mortar consists of lime mixed with sand and water. So, why did they use "slime?" What kind of "slime" was this? Luther translates this with "earth resin" or "gum." The Hebrew Bible makes it very plain when it says, "...and bitumen served them as mortar." *Webster's Dictionary* defines bitumen as "asphalt of Asia Minor, used in ancient times as a cement and mortar."

Bitumen is related to oil, of which there is plenty in the Mideast.

Thus, two items were used to build a global society:

1) Bricks, uniformly made, were the building blocks.

2) Asphalt was the adhesive that held the blocks together.

The second substance, which we have just identified, is a derivative of oil. Today, it is the substance that holds the industrialized world together: oil!

Oil's importance became painfully evident after 1973 when Egypt and Syria attacked Israel on their most holy day, Yom Kippur. Because the U.S.A. supported Israel, the Arab states punished the Western World, specifically the U.S.A., by quadrupling the price of oil. As a result, an economic catastrophe shook the entire world in the 70s and up into the 80s.

These two examples—the uniformity of bricks and adhesiveness of mortar—illustrate the connection between the Tower of Babel, Babylon, and the coming New World Order which will finally become Mystery Babylon.

Global World Already Exists
How is the world being united into a global society today? Through education! One key tool in the effort to educate for a one-world order is the presentation of the theory of evolution as fact, even though obviously it is *not* fact.

There are many more aspects regarding the uniting of the world, but we will not go into detail at this point, except to add that no one can deny that we are already living in a global society.

For example, through satellite communications, at any time, we can talk with almost anyone around the world.

This information explosion would have seemed incon-
ceivable just 50 years ago. Today's children are growing up
in an age of communication never known before. Some
young people who can barely read are already "surfing the
Internet," receiving information in seconds from anywhere
in the world.

If, for example, a college professor needed certain information which he heard was available somewhere in Hong
Kong, he had to undertake a time-consuming process of
research to obtain certain information.

Today, it's available instantaneously the world over to
anyone with access to the Internet. We don't need to bela-
bor this point further, for it is plainly understood that the
process toward global unity is in full swing today.

Religious Unity
It's necessary to point out one more item, however, regarding the people who built the Tower of Babel. Not only did
they speak one language, and obviously were united in politics and economy, but the reason for their unity was religion, as it is so clearly expressed in Genesis 11:4, "...let us
build us a city and a tower, whose top may reach unto
heaven...." It is doubtful that these intelligent people actually thought that they could reach the heavens of God
through their building. Surely they had enough sense and
education to know that it would be impossible since there
was no visible manifestation of such a place.

Based on the fact that all people at all times worship
something—whether it's a man-made object, animals, or
components of the universe such as the sun, moon and
stars—there is no doubt in my mind that "reaching unto
heaven" has a religious connotation. Thus, we must conclude that this "reaching unto heaven" was man's united
effort to bring forth his own salvation.

*great observation °

Self Esteem

Also, we notice quickly that this united effort included an ego trip: *"...Let us make us a name..."* testifies to that fact. We see that the religious aspect was mixed with politics and economy to glorify sinful man.

We know from Isaiah 14 that the Devil, called Lucifer, is the originator of man's preoccupation with self-image: *"For thou hast said in thine heart, I will ascend into heaven, I will exalt my throne above the stars of God: I will sit also upon the mount of the congregation, in the sides of the north:*

"I will ascend above the heights of the clouds; I will be like the most High" (Isaiah 14:13–14).

Satan surely has no problem with self-esteem. Today, he is fervently busy trying to reinforce this damnable notion of the need for self-esteem into the minds of millions the world over. It is the new gospel proclaimed to bring peace to troubled people. Having been in the ministry since 1968, I have yet to meet a person who claims to have a problem with self-esteem, who in reality is not excessively full of pride.

Although these people often claim that they don't think much of themselves and that they feel like losers with no self worth, during an extended counseling session, it becomes quickly apparent that they think more of themselves than they care to admit.

They are merely disappointed that "their value" has not become more obvious to those around them.

The Bible condemns self-esteem, and instead admonishes us to regard others more than ourselves, *"Let nothing be done through strife or vainglory; but in lowliness of mind let each esteem other better than themselves"* (Philippians 2:3). Thus, the low self-esteem theory is exposed as clever deceit from the proud one, Satan himself.

The Apostle Paul reinforces this fact to the Ephesians when he writes, *"For no man ever yet hated his own flesh;*

but nourisheth and cherisheth it, even as the Lord the church" (Ephesians 5:29).

Unified Deception
The Tower of Babel illustrates the first spirit of rebellion brought forth through the unity of the people.

This is also a picture of the last great world-wide rebellion against the living God.

Revelation 17:5 reads, *"And upon her forehead was a name written, MYSTERY, BABYLON THE GREAT, THE MOTHER OF HARLOTS AND ABOMINATIONS OF THE EARTH."*

Verse 3 of Revelation 18 identifies the world-wide political, economic, and religious unity, *"For all nations have drunk of the wine of the wrath of her fornication, and the kings of the earth have committed fornication with her, and the merchants of the earth are waxed rich through the abundance of her delicacies."*

Whether we read the Old or the New Testament, we find the Babylonian spirit running through the entire Scripture, showing us the progressive way of deception until the entire world will become unified.

Babylon the Conqueror
To better understand ancient Babylon, let's take a closer look at the time of Israel–Judah's demise.

In chapter 20, Jeremiah begins to prophesy about God's tool of judgment upon disobedient Judah, *"For thus saith the Lord, Behold, I will make thee a terror to thyself, and to all thy friends: and they shall fall by the sword of their enemies, and thine eyes shall behold it: and I will give all Judah into the hand of the king of Babylon, and he shall carry them captive into Babylon, and shall slay them with the sword"* (verse 4).

This was extremely difficult for the people of Israel to understand. They knew that God had chosen them to be a special nation above all others in the world, but now they faced defeat and deportation into a foreign land.

Surely, many of the Jews must have debated the validity of Jeremiah's prophecy. They remembered that it was the God of Israel who had led them out of Egypt, brought them into the Promised Land, established the kingdom under King David, built the glorious Temple under King Solomon, and did mighty things.

Such judgments must have been incomprehensible to the average Jewish person. From Jeremiah, we learn that the people indeed did not believe his words. They were holding desperately to past glories and could not see how their still-existing kingdom would be destroyed by enemy forces. But not believing in the Word of God causes blindness which then results in believing a lie and that is the greatest deception.

"Nebuchadnezzar My Servant"
Because of unbelief, Israel was incapable of seeing God's plan, which included His mercy in spite of the coming judgment. They were so occupied with "self" that it was impossible for them to recognize that God was actually on the side of the king of Babylon! Here we see how God includes a Gentile dictator to bring His plan to pass with His people.

It was the Lord who called Nebuchadnezzar "my servant." Read the words of Jeremiah 27:5–7, *"I have made the Earth, the man and the Beast that are upon the ground, by my great power and by my outstretched arm, and have given it unto whom it seemed meet unto me.*

"And now have I given all these lands into the hand of Nebuchadnezzar the king of Babylon, my servant; and the beasts of the field have I given him also to serve him.

"And all nations shall serve him, and his son, and his son's son, until the very time of his land come: and then many nations and great kings shall serve themselves of him."

Not only do we read that God had chosen Israel's enemy, Nebuchadnezzar, to be the ruler over His nation, but God pronounced severe judgment upon those who refused to obey him, *"And it shall come to pass, that the nation and kingdom which will not serve the same Nebuchadnezzar the king of Babylon, and that will not put their neck under the yoke of the king of Babylon, that nation will I punish, saith the LORD, with the sword, and with the famine, and with the pestilence, until I have consumed them by his hand"* (Jeremiah 27:8).

If Israel would have believed in the prophetic Word, then indeed their punishment would not have been so bad. Also, they would have recognized that within these terrible prophecies, God's grace was included.

The promise of a return to the land of Israel was part of it. But Israel continued to rebel against the living God and His messenger Jeremiah; thus, a terrible catastrophe came upon the people.

Modern Christian Rebellion
There seems to be a parallel rebellious spirit among Christians in our day. During the 1996 U.S. election, our office received an abundance of material from political activists.

Many letters came in, some of which were threatening. Christian political activists promised to change the national, moral and political fabric of America.

It was presumed that if Christians would run the country, an upright, just, and moral society could be established worthy of the name of Jesus.

A popular Christian television host proposed that such a revival would prepare the nation and the world for the Second Coming of Christ.

The blunt fact, however, is that we do not have any such promise in the Scripture. The church is the heavenly people of God and our task is made distinctively clear in the commandment of our exalted Lord, *"...Go ye into all the world, and preach the gospel to every creature"* (Mark 16:15).

Our relationship to the prevailing government is defined in Romans 13:1–7, *"Let every soul be subject unto the higher powers. For there is no power but of God: the powers that be are ordained of God.*

"Whosoever therefore resisteth the power, resisteth the ordinance of God: and they that resist shall receive to themselves damnation.

"For rulers are not a terror to good works, but to the evil. Wilt thou then not be afraid of the power? do that which is good, and thou shalt have praise of the same:

"For he is the minister of God to thee for good. But if thou do that which is evil, be afraid; for he beareth not the sword in vain: for he is the minister of God, a revenger to execute wrath upon him that doeth evil.

"Wherefore ye must needs be subject, not only for wrath, but also for conscience sake.

"For for this cause pay ye tribute also: for they are God's ministers, attending continually upon this very thing.

"Render therefore to all their dues: tribute to whom tribute is due; custom to whom custom; fear to whom fear; honour to whom honour"

And Titus 3:1–2 adds, *"Put them in mind to be subject to principalities and powers, to obey magistrates, to be ready to every good work,*

"To speak evil of no man, to be no brawlers, but gentle, shewing all meekness unto all men." These well-meaning

I have a definite problem here

Christians were actually fighting against the God of heaven, for the Bible says that *"...he removeth kings, and setteth up kings...."* All things are in the Lord's hand. He has the last say regarding kings, prime ministers, and presidents. These little insignificant people are no obstacle to the Lord.

But, when we who have been purchased with the precious blood of the Lord Jesus Christ mingle in the affairs which belong to the kingdom of this world, then we become part of the battle with "flesh and blood," and are hindered from fulfilling our task.

The language used against politicians before, during and after the 1996 election surpassed the most debased gutter language. Christians who, based on the Word of God, are supposed to be servants, meek and lowly, showing to all men the love of Christ, became ravaging wolves. Claiming to do the will of God, they were actually fighting with unlimited arrogance against the will of God. Some statisticians claim that over $800 million dollars were spent by Christian political activists in the election. Everything, however, was a loss. God chose Bill Clinton, although I have to admit I am not in favor of him.

[handwritten margin note: I'm seeing RED! A Republic is set up to put men in authority who seek the answers from God.]

A Warning for Christians

Israel's history gives us a serious lesson for our daily walk with the Lord. If the Lord permits you to go through trials and tribulations, it should not be your first priority to get out of them, or to fight desperately against anything that seems to oppose you. Rather, you should thrust yourself into the merciful arms of your Savior.

He has promised never to leave you nor forsake you, and He guarantees that He will not burden you with more than you can carry.

Paul wrote these words of comfort to the Corinthians, *"There hath no temptation taken you but such as is common*

to man: but God is faithful, who will not suffer you to be
tempted above that ye are able; but will with the temptation
also make a way to escape, that ye may be able to bear it"
(1st Corinthians 10:13).

Faith in the Midst of Destruction
Judah, with the remnant of Israel, did not believe this when
it was led into captivity. Jerusalem and the Temple were
burned and laid desolate. Everything the Prophet Jeremiah
proclaimed came to pass.

Some of the faithful Jews who believed in the God of
Israel recognized and confessed their sins.

It is of utmost importance that we take note of their true
spiritual attitude: They did not blame others, but themselves,
"And now, O our God, what shall we say after this? for we
have forsaken thy commandments,

"Which thou hast commanded by thy servants the
prophets, saying, The land, unto which ye go to possess it,
is an unclean land with the filthiness of the people of the
lands, with their abominations, which have filled it from one
end to another with their uncleanness.

"Now therefore give not your daughters unto their sons,
neither take their daughters unto your sons, nor seek their
peace or their wealth for ever: that ye may be strong, and
eat the good of the land, and leave it for an inheritance to
your children for ever.

"And after all that is come upon us for our evil deeds, and
for our great trespass, seeing that thou our God hast pun-
ished us less than our iniquities deserve, and hast given us
such deliverance as this;

"Should we again break thy commandments, and join in
affinity with the people of these abominations? wouldest not
thou be angry with us till thou hadst consumed us, so that
there should be no remnant nor escaping?

"O LORD God of Israel, thou art righteous: for we remain yet escaped, as it is this day: behold, we are before thee in our trespasses: for we cannot stand before thee because of this" (Ezra 9:10–15).

That was genuine repentance! Although the independent nations of Judah and Israel ceased to exist, and indeed the punishment was great, Ezra recognized God's mercy in the midst of judgment when he said, *"…Thou our God has punished us less than our iniquities deserve…"* (Ezra 9:13).

The Double Portion of Punishment

The punishment which threatened Israel was never applied to the full measure during the 70 years of captivity. Jeremiah's prophecy was not in vain, however. The grace of the Lord broke through, and the original pronouncement of a double portion of punishment did not take place during that time. We must recall verse 18 of Jeremiah 16:

"…I will recompense their iniquity and their sin double; because they have defiled my land, they have filled mine inheritance with the carcases of their detestable and abominable things."

The question we need to answer is, "When did Israel receive the double portion of punishment for their sins?"

From what we have seen so far, this double portion of punishment was not applied to the Jews before, during and after the Babylonian capture of Jerusalem and their subsequent return to Jerusalem 70 years later.

Neither do we find any evidence that Israel received a double portion for their sins from that time until the coming of the Messiah, the Lord Jesus Christ.

However, the Prophet Isaiah admonishes us to, *"Comfort ye, comfort ye my people, saith your God. Speak ye comfortably to Jerusalem, and cry unto her, that her warfare is accomplished, that her iniquity is pardoned: for she hath*

received of the LORD'S hand double for all her sins"
(Isaiah 40:1-2).

Isaiah was not speaking about the 70 years of captivity in
the land of Babylon, but he prophesied of the terrible catastrophes that would come upon Jerusalem and the Jews in
later years.

Some historians say that Jerusalem was destroyed and
rebuilt some 14 times, and that over 14 million Jews were
killed since the destruction of the Temple in A.D. 70 until
the Holocaust that ended in 1945.

I believe these facts constitute a "double" portion of
punishment!

Isaiah distinctly calls the nations of the world to comfort
the Jewish people: *"Speak ye comfortably to Jerusalem...."*
Why? Because *"...she hath received of the LORD'S hand
double for all her sins"* (Isaiah 40:2).

Under Roman Rule

About 500 years later, after Babylonian captivity, when
Israel's salvation arrived, when Jesus was born, the nation
 was totally unprepared for His coming, and according to
Scripture, they rejected and condemned Him to death.

At that time, the Jews were not in captivity, but were living in their own land under the jurisdiction of Rome.
Although they were a defeated nation, under the protective
custody of the Roman Empire, they lived relatively secure
in their own land, with certain limitations, not as a free and
independent nation. This is quite evident in the New
Testament.

After Jesus demonstrated His Messiahship with signs and
miracles, we read that many believed Him.

This caused the chief priest and the religious authorities
to be greatly concerned because they heard that He was
called the King of the Jews, *"Then gathered the chief priests*

and the Pharisees a council, and said, What do we? for this man doeth many miracles.

"If we let him thus alone, all men will believe on him: and the Romans shall come and take away both our place and nation" (John 11:47–48).

Here, we have evidence that a certain degree of liberty was available to the Jews in the land of Israel. If they continued to subject themselves to the infrastructure of the authority of Rome, they could live in reasonable peace and keep their identity as a nation. We also must point out that Jesus, during His ministry, never opposed the Roman occupation of the land of Israel. He surely was not a political activist. Actually, He endorsed the Roman government by plainly stating that the people should pay taxes because they were due to Caesar, *"...Render to Caesar the things that are Caesar's, and to God the things that are God's"* (Mark 12:17). Jesus' statement runs parallel to God the Father's statement about *"...Nebuchadnezzar the king of Babylon, my servant...."* We must see this clearly. Nebuchadnezzar was a pagan, an enemy of God, but God used him to fulfill His purpose with His people.

In effect, Jesus is saying, more or less, the same thing: "Caesar is in control. He collects taxes. Pay taxes to him. Don't worry about what's right or wrong in this matter. Subject yourself under the authority of God who uses Nebuchadnezzar (or Caesar) for His purpose."

Church and State

Very distinctly and definitely, He separated church and state. Of course, the argument may be put forth that "separation" of God and state led Israel to its ruin. That is indeed true, but this applies exclusively to Israel. They were chosen collectively as a nation; but, we from among the Gentiles are *individually* chosen.

[handwritten margin note: Jesus was not an enemy of Rome. The Pharisees killed Him because if they admitted He was the Messiah, they would have lost their jobs. This was the excuse they used.]

Each one who comes through faith in Jesus Christ is added to the church. Now, the believer, born-again of the Spirit of God, becomes a member of the Church of Jesus Christ. But, neither he nor his nation have any promises whatsoever, politically or geographically.

Let's emphasize this important point of distinction between Israel and the church. While the church does not have political and geographic promises, Israel, in contrast, is the very center of political and geographic promises!

Abraham's Blessing

The overwhelming majority of Bible-believing Christians would agree that the beginning of Israel's political and geographic promises is to be traced back to Abraham.

In Genesis 12, Abraham received a personal, national and global promise, *"Now the LORD had said unto Abram, Get thee out of thy country, and from thy kindred, and from thy father's house, unto a land that I will shew thee:*

"And I will make of thee a great nation, and I will bless thee, and make thy name great; and thou shalt be a blessing:

"And I will bless them that bless thee, and curse him that curseth thee: and in thee shall all families of the earth be blessed" (Genesis 12:1–3).

Please note: not simply "a nation," but "a great nation." This clearly has political connotation. But the personal blessing Abraham received is extended, not only to his family and nation, but to the entire world: *"...in thee shall all families of the earth be blessed."*

Before Abraham, God did not have a special chosen nation. He had not provided a special family, nor a national or global blessing to any human being.

Someone may now object and say, "Well, this blessing is just spiritual." But that is clearly contradicted by Genesis 13:14–18, *"And the LORD said unto Abram, after that Lot was separated from him, Lift up now thine eyes, and look from the place where thou art northward, and southward, and eastward, and westward:*

"For all the land which thou seest, to thee will I give it, and to thy seed for ever.

"And I will make thy seed as the dust of the earth: so that if a man can number the dust of the earth, then shall thy seed also be numbered.

"Arise, walk through the land in the length of it and in the breadth of it; for I will give it unto thee.

"Then Abram removed his tent, and came and dwelt in the plain of Mamre, which is in Hebron, and built there an altar unto the LORD."

Abraham was challenged by God to look around to the north, south, east and west, because this land was to be given to his descendants "forever." Again, God reemphasized the fact that His descendants would be multiplied greatly, and just to make sure, God commanded Abraham to take a Holy Land tour, *"...walk through the land in the length of it and in the breadth of it...."* For those who attempt to spiritualize the promises God gave to Abraham, they will have a difficult time explaining this Holy Land tour which took place physically in a geographic area. What were the borders of this land? Genesis 15:18 answers, *"...Unto thy seed have I given this land, from the river of Egypt unto the great river, the river Euphrates."* This eliminates, in a very defined manner, spiritualizing the promises to Abraham. God spoke to him about land, and identified the river of Euphrates and the river of Egypt. These are clear geographic areas identifiable even today.

Israel Requests Equality
Finally, when the nation of Israel was established in the Promised Land, the people of Israel rebelled against the

Lord God who had chosen them, by requesting a king so they would be like all the other nations.

In 1st Samuel 8:7, God answers Samuel, *"...they have not rejected thee, but they have rejected me, that I should not reign over them."*

God's original intention was to call a people for Himself, who would be holy and blameless, judging in righteousness, unifying the priestly and the royal line, thus uniting religion and politics. But the people divided religion and politics. Why? *"That we also may be like all the nations..."* (1st Samuel 8:20).

King Saul Acts As a Priest

After Samuel had anointed Saul as king over Israel, Saul attempted to force the unity between priest and king, religion and politics, *"And Saul said, Bring hither a burnt offering to me, and peace offerings. And he offered the burnt offering.*

"And it came to pass, that as soon as he had made an end of offering the burnt offering, behold, Samuel came; and Saul went out to meet him, that he might salute him" (1st Samuel 13:9–10).

How did Samuel react? *"...Thou hast done foolishly: thou hast not kept the commandment of the LORD thy God, which he commanded thee: for now would the LORD have established thy kingdom upon Israel for ever.*

"But now thy kingdom shall not continue: the LORD hath sought him a man after his own heart, and the LORD hath commanded him to be captain over his people, because thou hast not kept that which the LORD commanded thee..." (verses 13–14).

The man after God's heart was David. He was a special figure in Israel's history. He loved the Lord, and respected the law of God. His father-in-law, Saul, who became his most bitter enemy, was nevertheless the anointed of the Lord and David respected him to such an extent that he put his own life on the line.

Because David followed the Lord, he came very close to the priesthood, so that on one occasion, we actually read that David sacrificed, *"At that time when David saw that the Lord had answered him in the threshingfloor of Ornan the Jebusite, then he sacrificed there"* (1st Chronicles 21:28).

Monarchy and Religion Separated

In spite of the fact that David sinned against God greatly and became an adulterer and murderer, he truly repented and his heart was dedicated to the Lord. This became evident from his immediate confession after Nathan accused him of his sin. David answered, *"...I have sinned against the LORD..."* (2nd Samuel 12:13).

In Saul's case, we also see a confession, *"...I have sinned..."* but this was neither sincere nor unconditional. The verse continues, *"...yet honour me now, I pray thee, before the elders of my people, and before Israel..."* (1st Samuel 15:30). The monarchy and priesthood were divided and could no longer be reconciled.

This division took place long before Israel entered the Promised Land. The tribe of Levi was separated. Numbers 1:48–51 reads, *"For the LORD had spoken unto Moses, saying, Only thou shalt not number the tribe of Levi, neither take the sum of them among the children of Israel:*

"But thou shalt appoint the Levites over the tabernacle of testimony, and over all the vessels thereof, and over all things that belong to it: they shall bear the tabernacle, and all the vessels thereof; and they shall minister unto it, and shall encamp round about the tabernacle.

"And when the tabernacle setteth forward, the Levites shall take it down: and when the tabernacle is to be pitched,

the Levites shall set it up: and the stranger that cometh nigh shall be put to death."

A priest had to be of the tribe of Levi and only a priest could offer a sacrifice unto the Lord.

It was for that very reason God rejected King Saul, who was of the tribe of Benjamin, but took it upon himself to offer a sacrifice unto the Lord.

But, then we read the prophecy in Psalm 85, *"Surely his salvation is nigh them that fear him; that glory may dwell in our land.*

"Mercy and truth are met together; righteousness and peace have kissed each other.

"Truth shall spring out of the earth; and righteousness shall look down from heaven" (verses 9–11).

Reconciliation between the king and the priest was to come. This prophecy, however, was only fulfilled when the King of the Jews, the High Priest, of the order of Melchezidek, became the Lamb of God, who carried away the sins of the world.

As a result, those who believe in Him are the first fruits of the perfect unity between the King and the priests. Thus, we read in Revelation 1:6, *"And hath made us kings and priests unto God and his Father; to him be glory and dominion for ever and ever. Amen."* This verse is referring to the church.

Note, however, that nowhere will we find any indication that an earthly nation shall be established by these saints who have become "kings and priests" in order to bring forth righteousness, justice and peace on Earth now. Many have attempted to do so, but have failed miserably, and will do so in the future.

As we have seen from the beginning, God gave the Jews into the hands of Nebuchadnezzar, king of Babylon. He was to rule over them.

Sin Against the Temple

However, it is also apparent from the Scripture that the nation which had conquered Israel caused more affliction to the Jewish people than God intended. The Prophet Zechariah reveals this fact in chapter 1, verse 15,

"And I am very sore displeased with the heathen that are at ease: for I was but a little displeased, and they helped forward the affliction."

Because of the excesses of Babylon, God destroyed this mighty world empire, as described in Jeremiah chapter 51.

"Why," we may ask, "does God call the king of Babylon 'my servant' to execute His judgment upon His people Israel and then turn around and destroy Babylon?"

The answer is found in verse 11 of Jeremiah 51, *"...because it is the vengeance of the LORD, the vengeance of his temple."*

Babylon went to Israel under the authority of God to lead the Jews of Israel into captivity, but we do not read that God instructed them to destroy the Temple. This mistake and multiple others were repeated throughout the centuries against the Jewish people but were never authorized by God.

Jerusalem Protected

The king gave the following prophecy, *"And the God that hath caused his name to dwell there destroy all kings and people, that shall put to their hand to alter and to destroy this house of God which is at Jerusalem. I Darius have made a decree; let it be done with speed"* (verse 12).

This statement has far-reaching consequences, even into our day.

The old glorious Roman Empire, which was responsible for the destruction of Jerusalem and the Temple, also experienced destruction.

But there is more. Jerusalem today has become a bone of contention, not only between the Jews and the Arabs, but between the Jews and the entire world.

I have said it before, but must repeat myself because it is so important: There isn't one nation under God's sun which supports Israel's right and sovereignty over the entire Promised Land, according to the Biblical borders from the Euphrates River to the river of Egypt.

And no nation agrees that Jerusalem should be the undivided capital city under the sovereignty of the Jewish state.

Jerusalem, the End-Time Sign

Let's look at parallel prophetic utterances made by the Prophet Isaiah, and about 700 years later by John the Baptist.

Verse 3 of chapter 40 of Isaiah speaks of John the Baptist, *"The voice of him that crieth in the wilderness...."*

How do we know it was John the Baptist? John 1:23 gives us the answer. He testifies, *"I am the voice of one crying in the wilderness, Make straight the way of the Lord, as said the prophet Esaias."* Did Israel as a nation collectively respond? Of course not!

We also notice there was no echo from among the people to this message.

Even the prophet had to ask, *"...What shall I cry? All flesh is grass, and all the goodliness thereof is as the flower of the field"* (Isaiah 40:6). In plain words, the messenger was admitting defeat: "It is hopeless; we are nothing; all flesh is grass."

What happened next was 2,000 years of silence!

Then, in verse 9 of Isaiah 40, we begin to see that this Scripture is prophetically directed to our time,

"O Zion, that bringest good tidings, get thee up into the high mountain; O Jerusalem, that bringest good tidings, lift

up thy voice with strength; lift it up, be not afraid; say unto the cities of Judah, Behold your God!"

The Prophet Isaiah is simply telling us that the great sign for the Jewish people and the world is Jerusalem.

During Jesus' time, Jerusalem was the cornerstone of the Jewish nation. From reading the New Testament, we see that they were rather proud of the city and the Temple.

Jesus, however, regarding the Temple and Jerusalem, prophesied that "not one stone would be left upon another."

How true that statement was became apparent when, in A.D. 70, the Romans destroyed the Temple and Jerusalem.

Today, almost 2,000 years later, Jerusalem has again become the cornerstone of the Jewish people, but a stumbling stone to all of the world.

We are in the midst of the conflict over Jerusalem in our day! The nations of the world have taken up their position. No country in the world stands behind Israel regarding their sovereignty over the Jewish capital city of Jerusalem. All, I repeat, *all* nations are against Israel's right to Jerusalem!

The Power of World Democracy
This time, the Jerusalem conflict is not limited to the Jews or the Roman Empire, but the entire world. Under the auspices of democracy, every nation is automatically involved.

Let's make a comparison with the building of the Tower of Babel, where the people were united in their effort to create their own salvation. Today, although it is not obvious, the nations of the world again are united against God and, therefore, they must create their own way to "reach unto heaven."

Someone may now ask, "How is the world united against God?" There are multiple answers to that question, but to say it briefly, the world goes in the opposite direction of God's prepared way.

The Bible says, *"...God was in Christ, reconciling the world unto himself, not imputing their trespasses unto them; and hath committed unto us the word of reconciliation"* (2nd Corinthians 5:19). Reconciliation with God is unity. Anything else is rebellion against the living God.

We see the beginning of the terror of Babylon, which is expressed through the unity of the world of nations, under the leadership of world democracy. Who can oppose democracy today? It is impossible. It has become the official political system of the globe and woe unto anyone who opposes it.

I must emphasize that I am not against democracy. The opposite is true. I think it is the best system because it guarantees more liberty, prosperity and human rights to people who are governed by it than under any other system. But that fact should never blind our eyes to the coming global danger of world democracy.

In the coming years, this fact will be much more evident as the world's most populous nation, China, becomes more democratic year-by-year. China's economic system today can no longer be considered communistic; it is becoming increasingly capitalistic. It is achieving an astonishing rate of growth that is stunning the rest of the world.

I repeat: All political philosophies will be integrated into the new world democracy, under the theme now expressed in the famous words of the U.S. Constitution: "We the people...."

Terror of Democracy

What is the terror of democracy? It is Mystery Babylon, the unseen, unnoticed power of the enemy who is uniting the nations of the world with peace, security, and prosperity.

What this means is that the new world order is going to produce an even more sophisticated economy under a more refined democratic system that will astonish the world. No one can deny the unbelievable progress that has been made, the Western World particularly, in the last 100 years.

When we compare our economic position to that of 30, 50, 80, or 200 years ago, we quickly conclude that we are much better off than ever before. Never have we had so much free time, worked so little, and had so much luxury than we have today.

But men with greedy spirits continue to lament and complain. They want more. Therefore, conditions will continue to improve. The nations will get richer; poverty will be reduced even more; and finally, I believe crime will be limited drastically by new measures governments the world-over will take, using modern crime-preventing electronics.

Peaceful Babylon
The terror of Babylon does not express itself in oppression, poverty, crime, and brutality, but in peace, security, and prosperity. The people who built the Tower of Babel were doing well. They spoke one language. Communication, therefore, was perfect. They were politically united. The people were in charge and they had a tremendous economic program. But underlying all this success was the desire for self-salvation. That, my dear friends, is the "terror of Babylon."

The "terror of Babylon" is also the conviction of man that he can produce salvation through his own established peace and prosperity. This was equally true at the judgment of Noah's flood. Men were doing well, eating and drinking, marrying and getting married, buying and selling. There was great prosperity, and no doubt, they had established their own homespun religion. Thus, they did not heed the Word of God which Noah preached. That, too, was the "terror of Babylon."

Successful Babylon

Let us identify Mystery Babylon from another observation point, which besides peace, includes success. The Babylon we read about in Revelation 18:3 is real, *"For all nations have drunk of the wine of the wrath of her fornication, and the kings of the earth have committed fornication with her, and the merchants of the earth are waxed rich through the abundance of her delicacies."*

The extreme success of world democracy, as reported in Revelation 13, will open the door for Mystery Babylon to take over a willing world.

By now, the reader will understand that Mystery Babylon, world democracy and Antichrist belong together. One cannot be without the other. The spirit of Antichrist was already present at the beginning of the church. John said, *"...even now are there many antichrists...."* The power of the people, which finds its roots in the Greek and Roman democracy, and has now developed into a democracy we are familiar with, is just another foundation stone toward the building of Mystery Babylon, which the Antichrist will finally take over.

I have never believed that the Antichrist and his power structure will come with force, destroying all opposition and establishing his reign of terror on Earth. This is contrary to the teaching of the Scripture, which emphasizes that he will come in through peaceful deception.

The Prophet Daniel identifies the Antichrist and his deception repeatedly. He writes: *"...by peace shall destroy many...he shall come in peaceably, and obtain the kingdom by flatteries"* (Daniel 8:25; 11:21).

"He shall enter peaceably even upon the fattest places of the province..." (verse 24).

His practical success is revealed in verse 27, *"...and they shall speak lies at one table...."*

Later on, the Apostle Paul confirms this tendency when he writes, *"Even him, whose coming is after the working of Satan with all power and signs and lying wonders,*

"And with all deceivableness of unrighteousness..." (2nd Thessalonians 2:9–10). This man is also the epitome of self-esteem, *"...he shall magnify himself in his heart..."* (Daniel 8:25). And in Daniel 11:36, *"...he shall exalt himself, and magnify himself above every god...."*

No wonder that Revelation says, *"And all that dwell upon the Earth shall worship him..."* (Revelation 13:8).

So, the Antichrist will come with flattery and lies, through deception. What is deception? It is something that we assume takes place but actually does not. It looks like truth but it is a lie. It seems like it is light but it is darkness.

We see the deceptive power structure of the Antichrist in verse 4 of Revelation 13, *"And they worshipped the dragon which gave power unto the Beast: and they worshipped the Beast, saying, Who is like unto the Beast? who is able to make war with him?"*

The people of the world will be totally amazed at this wonderful, glorious, extremely successful new world system that will implement a form of righteousness which will correspond to the corrupt nature of man, which is "self."

Gladly the people will lay down all their honor and bring it to the Antichrist, and the whole world will worship him.

Hitler—Forerunner of Antichrist

How deception worked in Germany for the masses of the people seems to be a mystery to the rest of the world. But the deception was nearly perfect. Even after the total collapse of Germany, support for Hitler was still strong. He was democratically elected by the people.

Credit was given to him for resurrecting Germany to a prosperous, vibrant society, which had become poverty-stricken under the burden of the First World War and the sanctions imposed by the Treaty of Versailles.

From the hundreds, if not thousands, of people I have spoken to, the testimony has been the same: Hitler established law and order. Prosperity replaced poverty; crime was virtually eliminated; pride in the nation was at an all-time high.

Only rarely have I met someone who had a deep hate for Hitler and his system.

One such person was a German engineer, Wolfgang Duwe, whom I met in Melbourne, Australia. A convinced atheist, he despised Hitler and his Bible-quoting speeches.

My wife's grandmother was a practicing occultist. She hated Hitler passionately. Even before the war, she would say, "Wait, you will yet see what you get out of this bloodhound."

Criminals trembled at the sight of Hitler and homosexuals were eliminated along with the Jews. Religious cults, such as Jehovah's Witnesses, Mormons, and others, were forbidden to assemble. The doors of the lodges of the Freemasons were locked. Abortion was outlawed, and Bible reading and prayer were part of the school's curriculum.

How did born-again Christians react? My mother-in-law, who went home to be with the Lord in 1989, testified many times, "We were on our knees thanking and praising God for sending us such a leader." Only later, when the persecution of Jews became more obvious, mother asked her closest Christian friend secretly, "Could Hitler be the Antichrist?"

To summarize, "the terror of Babylon" is manifesting itself today in our society through peace, security, and prosperity.

In the success of our free democratic system lurks the unrecognized danger of deception which is coming in the days ahead.

Our Unchanged Commission

What are we to do in view of the coming "terror of Babylon"? We should exclusively obey the Word of God, *"Go ye into all the world and preach the gospel to every creature."*

Opposition against a democratically elected government will fail miserably and we will only add to our suffering, which then is self-inflicted, and will not, therefore, bring forth fruit for eternity and for the glory of our Lord Jesus.

Let us, therefore, as we see these things come to pass, more willingly than ever, look to Him, the author and finisher of our faith. He said, *"I am...the first and the last,"* (Revelation 22:13), and it is He who *"has made us kings and priests unto God and his Father"* (Revelation 1:6).

As "kings," we don't have to be discouraged or downcast, but we can act uprightly in a royal manner even among a crooked and perverse generation.

As "priests," we present the sins of the people to God and ask for forgiveness. We don't condemn others!

It is moving to read how the faithful servant of the Lord, Daniel, acted in the presence of God. When reading Daniel 9, we notice that he repeatedly identified himself with the sins of his people, *"O Lord, to us belongeth confusion of face, to our kings, to our princes, and to our fathers, because we have sinned against thee"* (Daniel 9:8).

"We have sinned"... *"Neither have we hearkened unto thy servants the prophets"*...*"Righteousness belongeth unto thee, but unto us confusion of faces"*...*"We have sinned against thee"*...*"We have rebelled against him"*...*"Neither have we obeyed the voice of the Lord our* God" (verses 5–10).

Such a priestly attitude is urgently needed today. We don't need political activists; we don't need those who walk the streets in protest against the evils in our society.

What we need is a spirit of repentance among Christians. We need brothers and sisters who are willing to sacrifice their lives for the Lord's sake and willing to become "priests" for the sins of the nation.

We must execute our office as "kings" and "priests," remaining in the presence of the eternal God through our Lord Jesus Christ, asking Him to give us the courage to hold onto Him alone and not deviate from the commandment of our exalted Lord, *"Go ye into all the world and preach the gospel to every creature."*

When we fail to do that, we are moving ourselves into the territory of the "terror of Babylon."

Euro—the currency of the European Union

CHAPTER SEVEN

Babylon, Europe and the World

Summary

This chapter pinpoints the continuous development toward a united world. It shows how Europe is reestablishing her philosophical dominance worldwide in an attempt to replace God's chosen nation of Israel, which is destined to rule the Earth.

T*hus saith the LORD, the Holy One of Israel, and his Maker, Ask me of things to come concerning my sons, and concerning the work of my hands command ye me"* (Isaiah 45:11).

We do well to remember this Scripture, considering all that we hear, read and see in our day, particularly regarding the events that are happening in the Middle East.

What's Not Important

It's not of basic importance that Iraq, under the leadership of Saddam Hussein, violates agreements with the United Nations or threatens its neighbors. Neither is it of importance how the U.S. reacts, whether by sending troops or bombing military targets.

These things, and many others we've not listed, are only the result of God's purpose to fulfill His prophetic Word. When we talk about the past, present, and future, we must do what we're admonished to do in the introductory Scripture: *"...Ask me of things to come...."*

Politicians Insignificant

It's of little or no importance what President Boris Yeltsin, President Bill Clinton or Pope John Paul II say, or don't say.

Even the actions of all nations combined are actually trivial when compared with God's calling of the nation of Israel. Isaiah 40:17 reads, *"All nations before him are as nothing; and they are counted to him less than nothing, and vanity."* This Scripture should settle our minds once and for all regarding the importance of news events propagated so impressively through our news media.

Not only are the nations *"nothing,"* but they're *"less than nothing,"* according to the Bible.

I think we can understand quickly that as children of God, we have only one authority: our Father, who is the Creator of heaven and Earth, and the Son, the Lord Jesus Christ, who defeated the powers of darkness when He cried out on Calvary's cross, *"It is finished!"*

Heavenly Perspectives
This means we must learn to observe world-shaking events from eternal perspectives. Never must we underestimate our position in Christ Jesus or forget what Ephesians 2:6 says, *"And* [he] *hath raised us up together, and made us sit together in heavenly places in Christ Jesus."*

To back up this Scripture, let's also read Philippians 3:20, *"For our conversation is in heaven; from whence also we look for the Saviour, the Lord Jesus Christ."* We're complete in Him!

These two Scriptures, however, raise questions in our minds because they seem contradictory.

From a scientific point of view, we're neither sitting with Christ in heavenly places, nor are our "conversations" or "walks" in heaven yet. It bids us, therefore, to amplify the meaning of these Scriptures.

To understand this important item better, let me give a couple of examples:

It's an indisputable fact that the sun rises in the east. During the day, we can measure scientifically, with the most exact instrument, the movement of the sun rising in the east and setting in the west.

But, this "indisputable fact" becomes invalid the moment we travel outside the atmosphere of Earth. We then see that the Earth turns on its own axis. The sun doesn't revolve around the Earth. Scientific facts apply only in their own place and in proper relationship.

Weight is another matter that helps illustrate this point. We can prove the phenomenon of weight scientifically. Let's say I weigh 70 kilos (155 pounds). This "weight" is an established fact. It may vary slightly, depending on the precision of the scale. However, if I were to take that same scale and somehow get to the moon, my scientific established weight would decrease to only 11.5 kilos (26 pounds).

Right now, while you read these lines, you are on Earth, bound by the physical laws of this planet, but in spirit, you're a child of God. Your citizenship is in heaven, and you're already in His presence. Through rebirth, you've become an eternal person. Past, present and future are one.

Old Babylon Confronts Mystery Babylon

When we ask the question, "What's happening today in Iraq?" we must look at the answer from a spiritual and eternal perspective. We can summarize the answer in one short sentence, "Old Babylon is opposing Mystery Babylon."

Today's Babylon is called Iraq, where ancient Babylon was located. For several decades now, we've been witnessing a military conflict in ancient Babylon, the Persian Gulf region.

On the 22nd of September, 1980, open warfare began between Iraq (Babylon) and Iran (Persia), over the Shatt al-Arab Waterway. This war was very costly to Iran and nearly led the nation to bankruptcy. Estimates of casualties ranged from 450,000 to one million. The conflict lasted eight years, until September 1988, when a U.N.-sponsored conference led to a ceasefire. No clear winner emerged.

From 1988—1990, Iraq, under the leadership of Saddam Hussein, continued an arms buildup, which provoked widespread international criticism.

On August 2nd, 1990, about 120,000 Iraqi troops invaded Kuwait and later annexed the country. Therefore, the United Nations eventually authorized the U.S. to lead a multi-national attack with the aim to oust Iraq from Kuwait.

It took almost six months to assemble 500,000 troops from thirteen countries for the attack, which began on January 16, 1991.

The only country in great danger was Israel, which was threatened with chemical attacks.

During the Gulf War, Israel nervously noticed the ineffectiveness of the Allied invasion. While the Western press proclaimed great success, for Israel it was a great disappointment. Any war lasting more than just a couple of weeks would have been devastating for Israel. Furthermore, the much-praised Patriot missiles scored no hits over Israel against Saddam's Scuds. Again, Israel was reminded that no guarantee from any nation can protect them.

Israel stayed out of the conflict, but that's not to say that it will do so in the future.

Why is Israel so important? Because Israel is the center of God's plan in world history.

It was in Israel that God, through His Son, the Lord Jesus Christ, reconciled the world unto Himself. He died in Israel, was buried there, arose victoriously on the third day there, ascended into heaven from there, and according to the prophetic Word, will one day return there.

The geographic location of Israel is very important. Babylon lies to the east of Israel and Mystery Babylon, the new world empire, is primarily situated to the west. *Ahah!*

Unfulfilled Prophecy

Looking back at our introductory Scripture, Isaiah 45:11, we notice that our question about the future should be directed to *"...the Holy One of Israel."* He invites us to be concerned about *"my sons"* and *"the work of my hands."* We can't understand the past, present, or future if we don't understand the work God is doing with, in and through His people, Israel.

The First Census

In order for God to cause the fulfillment of prophecy, He may have to use the whole world to do it.

Let's see an example in Luke 2:1 where God uses the world to fulfill His Word: *"And it came to pass in those days, that there went out a decree from Caesar Augustus, that all the world should be taxed."*

Why was the whole world taxed? We must point out that the word "taxed" doesn't mean the same today as it did a few hundred years ago. This "taxing" involved *counting* the people. It was a census. Caesar was counting his subjects!

The whole world then was "in motion." Every person had to go back to the place where he was born to be counted, to be enrolled.

The highways were filled with people and animals. There was commotion everywhere and surely many complained and grieved.

"What's the purpose of all this? Why do we have to go to our town of birth and register? Why can't this be done in writing, or sent by a courier?"

We can imagine that the prices for horses and donkeys were skyrocketing; lodging places were filled to capacity.

What was the purpose? There was one distinct reason: Micah 5:2 proclaims, *"But thou, Bethlehem Ephratah, though thou be little among the thousands of Judah, yet out of thee shall he come forth unto me that is to be ruler in Israel; whose goings forth have been from of old, from everlasting."*

This was all in preparation of the birth of the Messiah, although the world at large—even the Bible students (Pharisees, Sadducees and Scribes)—had no idea what was happening. The Messiah of Israel, the Savior of the world, had to be born in the little town of Bethlehem to fulfill Bible prophecy!

But, where was Mary, the mother of Jesus? In Nazareth! That's about 145 km (87 miles) north of Bethlehem. Jesus couldn't be born in Nazareth; He had to be born in Bethlehem, according to the Scriptures.

Therefore, to accommodate the birth of Jesus in Bethlehem in agreement with the prophetic Word, the whole Roman Empire was on the move!

Saddam's Babylon

Now that we understand the reason for events and conflicts, let us take a closer look at Saddam's Iraq.

From a historical perspective, Saddam Hussein had some valid reasons for his eight-year war with Iran, and also, the later invasion of Kuwait, because the areas fought over really belonged to ancient Babylon.

The following analysis may offend some, especially if misunderstood, so let me make myself clear: I abhor the brutal behavior of Saddam Hussein, and most surely sympathize with the unfortunate people of Kuwait who lost their country temporarily.

But, as a believer in the Lord Jesus Christ, I'm a citizen of heaven and I'm obligated to view world events from the perspective of Bible prophecy.

The events predicted in the Scripture will happen. The question is, "Who will implement them?" Jesus said, *"...for it must needs be that offences come; but woe to that man by whom the offence cometh"* (Matthew 18:7). Had it not been Saddam Hussein, it would have been someone else. The reawakening of Babylon is a prophetic requirement.

Neither Saddam Hussein nor anyone else can change the general course of the world.

Only He who has the past, the present, and the future of the world in His hands can change things. He'll bring His Word to pass in the finest detail!

Every Country Established by Force

Again, I reemphasize the fact that I'm not a friend of Saddam Hussein; I deplore his acts of violence. But, truthfully, we can't deny that in recent history, most of the nations have acted just as Saddam Hussein has.

We can start from the top of Canada and travel down to the very tip of Argentina, and find that all these nations were established with the sword or the gun! That was equally the case with the continent of Australia.

What about Russia? She swallowed country after country by force and established the Union of Soviet Socialist Republics. Now these borders are changing again, and often by warfare.

Britain conquered over 25% of the world by force. Those who opposed it were brutally oppressed and often killed. Governments were installed—not by the indigenous people—but by the foreign colonial force from Europe. The people were forced to become subjects of the little island kingdom of Great Britain.

What about the European countries? The borders between the various nations were established by force. That was the norm, the unwritten law, accepted by all who were the winners in a conflict. Therefore, Saddam Hussein was only doing what most other countries had done beforehand.

Most nations got away with it until Israel arose. There, in Israel, for the first time, the victor in war wasn't permitted to deal "justly" with the defeated enemies.

The nations of the world, who themselves had conquered territory by force, condemned Israel and pressured the Jews to surrender the land they had taken from the enemies as a matter of national survival.

We realize that we can't analyze these occurrences from a political view, but we must examine them from a spiritual perspective.

God allows the nations of the world to condemn Iraq because all nations, as well as all individuals, will one day have to condemn themselves out of their own mouths!

Again, we have no sympathy for Saddam Hussein, but when honestly analyzed, we must confess that our own nation is guilty of the very same crimes which we condemn others for.

Reappearance of Israel

The events we've witnessed in the past few decades and which we see happening today in frightening proportions are nothing other than the revelation of the dark powers that were hidden for thousands of years and must now become visible because of Israel's reappearance.

Before 1948, the whole Middle East was at relative ease. The European nations, as colonial powers, divided large and small territories among themselves, establishing nations such as Iraq, Kuwait, Syria, Lebanon, and Jordan, to mention a few.

Although conflicts erupted in many places, there was no major threat of an international war.

With the appearance of Israel, however, everything suddenly changed. Israel became the concern of the nations.

We must understand that all nations are ruled by the god of this world, the prince of the power of darkness.

With no exceptions, all nations, good or evil, are under the influence of Satan, as 2nd Corinthians 4:4 assures us, *"In whom the god of this world hath blinded the minds of them which believe not, lest the light of the glorious gospel of Christ, who is the image of God, should shine unto them."*

Therefore, the moment Israel came on the scene, the activity against Israel had to become visible.

This was also the case when Jesus, the Light of the world, came to Israel.

When He appeared, the powers of darkness had to identify themselves.

In one case, a man possessed with evil spirits protested,
*"...What have we to do with thee, Jesus, thou Son of God?
art thou come hither to torment us before the time?"*
(Matthew 8:29).

The coming of Jesus exposed the darkness of Satan, just
as the coming of Israel exposes the position of the nations
under the power of darkness.

The Four Angels of War

As I mentioned earlier, the military conflicts involving
Babylon (Iraq) began on September 22, 1980. The war
which lasted eight years was limited between Iraq and Iran,
primarily over the control of the Shatt Al-Arab Waterway in
southern Iraq at the mouth of the Euphrates River.

I believe this has relevance to the prophecies found in
Revelation 9, where we read the following in verses 14–15,
*"Saying to the sixth angel which had the trumpet, Loose the
four angels which are bound in the great river Euphrates.*

*"And the four angels were loosed, which were prepared
for an hour, and a day, and a month, and a year, for to slay
the third part of men."*

Thus, the loosening of the four angels of war begins in
the territory of old Babylon.

This shouldn't be surprising because not only is ancient
Babylon where the history of the times of the Gentiles
began, but, as we'll see later, the history of the Gentile
nations will end with Mystery Babylon.

Four Gentile Empires at War

It's significant that all four former world empires have been
involved in armed conflicts in the last few decades. We
already mentioned:

1) Iraq (Babylon) and

2) Iran (Medo-Persian Empire). This war ended when a U.N. conference led to a ceasefire in 1988.

3) Greece, the third Gentile world empire, was involved in an armed conflict against Turkey in 1974, over the isles of Cyprus. This conflict continues and is the main reason Turkey has been refused entry into the exclusive club of the European Union.

4) The conflict between Babylon and Mystery Babylon (Western World under the Roman system) started on August 2, 1990, when 120,000 Iraqi troops invaded and annexed neighboring Kuwait.

That invasion was met by universal disapproval, which was highlighted by the United Nations Security Council condemnation.

Trained personnel, with superior equipment and technology, made the Iraqis realize immediately that victory over the Allied forces was impossible.

Little resistance was experienced, although the media overplayed the scenario by comparing it to a World War which never materialized. This "war" was quickly settled with Iraqi forces surrendering.

Europe Leads the World

This conflict, as we've already said, involved Babylon and the new world empire called Mystery Babylon.

Someone may now ask, "What's the new world empire?"

Answer: The Western World! To be exact, Roman law and civilization are responsible for the success of Europe, which has conquered virtually the whole world.

We must point out here that of the world's five continents, two of them—America (North and South) and
Australia—are primarily the result of European settlers who
conquered the land, subdued it, and established political
identities, based on Roman laws.

Asia and Africa, the remaining two continents, can only
function economically, politically and financially under the
European system. To summarize, Roman democratic civilization is the cornerstone of the fourth, and last (fifth)
Gentile world empire. We often overlook the fact that the
fourth world empire, Rome, can't be compared to the three
previous Gentile world empires, because the Bible says,
"...the fourth kingdom...shall be diverse from all kingdoms..." (Daniel 7:23), and that the Roman system will last
until the Second Coming of Christ, when His feet stand on
the Mount of Olives.

This should be enough to show that since the resurrection
of the nation of Israel in 1948, all four former world empires
have been reawakened through military conflicts.

The latest conflict proved that the world can be united,
thus, preparing the nations of the world to be led by one
leader. Therefore, the whole event can be considered a
rehearsal for the coming Battle of Armageddon. However,
this battle won't happen because of Saddam Hussein and his
aspirations to rebuild Babylon; rather, it will happen
because of Israel.

The Abundant Treasures of Babylon
The Prophet Jeremiah writes more about Babylon than other
prophets put together. In chapter 51, the word "Babylon"
occurs 36 times. Please take time to read the chapter to better understand the following analysis.

You'll notice the similarity in judgment upon Babylon in
ancient time and the events which have happened in our

time. Verse 13 reads, *"O thou that dwellest upon many waters, abundant in treasures, thine end is come, and the measure of thy covetousness."*

The "waters" are exactly why Iraq was at war with Iran for eight years. Saddam Hussein claims the eastern coast of the Gulf of Persia as Iraq's historical territory. This is true, for it belonged to Babylon of old.

What about "abundant treasures?" Oil is the key to the world's industry. The thirst for oil from below unites the nations which stand in opposition to the nation God has chosen: Israel! No wonder that oil is rarely found in Israel. The oil from above, however, unites the Jews into one nation, and also unites the Church of Jesus Christ, because the oil from above pictures the Holy Spirit.

The true church, composed of those who are born-again of the Spirit of God, realize their roots. We're *"...grafted contrary to nature into the good olive tree..."* (Romans 11:24).

We, from among the Gentiles, haven't replaced Israel, but the Bible says, *"...the Gentiles have been made partakers of their [Israel's] spiritual things..."* (Romans 15:27).

But, if we are outside the faith, we're also outside everything that belongs to Israel, *"...being aliens from the commonwealth of Israel, and strangers from the covenants of promise, having no hope, and without God in the world"* (Ephesians 2:12).

Only those who are saved can claim the next verse: *"But now in Christ Jesus ye who sometimes were far off are made nigh by the blood of Christ"* (verse 13).

Now, we've become *"...fellow-heirs, and of the same body and partakers of his promise in Christ by the gospel"* (Ephesians 3:6). During these last few decades, I have sensed the unity among born-again believers more and more.

But the false spirit is also at work, gathering all of organized "churchianity" into one camp in opposition to the true Gospel. We plainly see how the Bible is increasingly disregarded. Meanwhile, the Holy Spirit is at work, refining and preparing the spotless bride for the Bridegroom. That's the work of the oil from above.

I must stress that all nations, without exception, are moving to the point of utter rebellion against the God of heaven. The final conflict will happen in Israel. It's called the Battle of Armageddon!

The nations of the world will always stand in opposition to God's plan. Thus, we read in Jeremiah 51:27, *"Set ye up a standard in the land, blow the trumpet among the nations, prepare the nations against her..."*

The assembling of the nations happened in 1991 against Iraq, but as I said, it was only a rehearsal for what's still to come.

The Fourth Empire

The scenario we've witnessed in this fight between Iraq and the world has cast a shadow before us so that we can better understand what Daniel wrote, *"Thus he said, The fourth beast shall be the fourth kingdom upon Earth, which shall be diverse from all kingdoms, and shall devour the whole Earth, and shall tread it down, and break it in pieces"* (Daniel 7:23).

The previous three Gentile world empires—Babylon, Medo-Persia, and Greece—could be identified, pictured by animals—lion, bear and leopard—but not the fourth one because this last empire *"...shall be diverse from all kingdoms."* That means there's no comparison in the history of humanity. This fourth kingdom won't be limited to Rome or Europe, but it will include the whole Earth, for it *"...shall devour the whole Earth."*

That's the problem with Democracy. It evolves into tyranny ruled by a dictator

BABYLON, EUROPE, AND THE WORLD   163

We're reminded that virtually the whole world today is operating under one political system: democracy. Only China and a couple of little countries are ruled by the communist system.

As we can already see, China may be communistic in philosophy, but it's definitely capitalistic in its practice. Inevitably, therefore, China will succumb to the dictates of democracy.

I'm fully aware that this is a strong statement, "China will succumb to the dictates of democracy." Based on our understanding, we'd rather say, "China will be liberated by the freedom of democracy!"

However, I'd say that both statements are valid. The play on words isn't important because the result is the same: democracy will rule the world.

tyranny

Early on, this global empire will appear to be very benevolent and successful, but in line with Scripture, the end will be the greatest catastrophe man has ever experienced. Man, in rebellion against God, will try to produce his own peace and prosperity without the God of the Bible.

We must remind ourselves that although we're democratically-minded, it was democracy which was the driving force behind the building of the Tower of Babel, symbolizing rebellion against the living God.

It was the spirit of democracy which caused Israel to deviate from God's plan when the Israelites requested a king so they'd be equal with all the nations around them.

And surely, it was the masses of the people, the opinion of the majority, a democratic action that condemned Jesus to the cross. *"...The chief priest and elders persuaded the multitude...They all say unto him, Let him be crucified"* (Matthew 27:20,22).

Not by laws

I share with you now the profound statement of the famous British leader, Winston Churchill, who once said,

"Democracy is the worst form of government, but it is the best
we have."

thats why we were a Republic

Let's reemphasize that the fourth kingdom is the last one
and it will be different from all others. Daniel 7:7 reads,
*"After this I saw in the night visions, and behold a fourth
beast, dreadful and terrible, and strong exceedingly; and it
had great iron teeth: it devoured and brake in pieces, and
stamped the residue with the feet of it: and it was diverse
from all the Beasts that were before it; and it had ten horns."*
Notice the words, *"...diverse from all the Beasts that were
before it...."*

The Negative Power

We do well to add an explanation to the words "beast";
"dreadful"; "terrible"; "strong exceedingly"; "great iron
teeth"; "devoured"; "brake in pieces"; and "stamped the
residue." These words have very negative connotations.

If we were to seek an example of such a horrible character in history, we probably would point to Hitler, whose
ideas were the major contributing factor to the Second
World War, which cost over fifty million lives. Hitler was
responsible for the wanton slaughter of six million Jews
throughout Europe. When we think along those lines, we're
correct, but only partly. Let me stress this strongly: The negative description we've just read in Daniel 7 is only the
result of the success of the fourth beast.

Under Hitler, Germany experienced remarkable prosperity and success; national pride was at an all-time high. So it
will be with the last global empire when the world follows
the successful model established by the fourth beast.

Sometimes we overlook the fact that we're already experiencing peace and prosperity at unheard-of levels. Too
often, our view is obscured by the negative reporting of the

news media, which constantly highlights death and destruction, crime and perversion, military conflicts and natural catastrophes, and many other tragic events that take place daily.

Life on Earth Getting Better? Or Worse?

Our natural tendency is to be influenced by these negative news reports, and become convinced that life on Earth is getting worse. The older generation will confirm this statement: "We never heard so much bad news as we do today." That, of course, is true. But, from another perspective, it is wrong. Why? Because today, we hear the news almost instantly from around the world.

A hundred or more years ago, the only news that reached the population was local or old news. Anything that happened in Europe took three, four, or five weeks until publication in America.

Even fifty years ago, news didn't travel very quickly, and when it reached the U.S.A., it was already old. The prime mode of contact was the telex machine upon which one had to key every letter on a typewriter-style keyboard, which was then wired to a distant spot. Such communication was very costly and only important news, largely abbreviated, could be sent.

Today, through satellite communication and the Internet, we have instant global access. The result is that we have the latest news from around the world. The media must now present the news *selectively* because of the huge mountain of news that's available daily. The question is, "What criteria must be used to pick news?" Answer: News must contain an element of excitement or drama.

Rarely will you hear or read news about a pastor who has spent nights in prayer with a sick person or the neighbor who has sacrificed much of his time and income to help another who has fallen into misfortune. Such reports don't sell papers or magazines. Neither will they boost the ratings of the broadcast program. Such reports are usually ignored.

Why am I mentioning all this? To stress that we must learn to read and understand the news. Anyone would be hard pressed to prove statistically that the United States, for example, is worse off today than it ever was. Yes, we do have danger and crimes, accidents and natural catastrophes, but those things are generally the fabric of any nation.

The difference today is that we hear instantly about fires raging in Oregon, a flash flood in Mexico, a dangerous storm sweeping Europe, or a tornado touchdown a thousand miles from our home.

Therefore, if we were to compare today's peace and prosperity with the past, we'd quickly agree that we're now more secure than ever before.

This is equally true for the liberties we enjoy and definitely the case where prosperity is concerned. Never have Americans been as rich as they are today. Never before have we had as many luxuries in our ownership and never before have Americans been able to buy, for a week's wages, as many goods as we can today.

Peace and prosperity are a reality today and, based on my understanding of the prophetic Word, it will increase to the point that the world will exclaim "Peace and safety!"

The Future Is Now
Think with me for a moment: Earlier, the threat to world peace was communism, but now that has been taken out of the way and democracy is ruling. Free-market business, the method of getting wealth, is spreading across the world.

Therefore, we must understand that the negative descriptions we read of previously, such as "break in pieces" and "stamped the residue" refer to the destruction of those ideas and practices that are based on tradition, heritage, race and nationality. They will be destroyed, but result in prosperity.

These traditional ways are being "broken in pieces" and what's left is being "stamped" with the iron boot of democracy. No wonder that "traditional family values" are being displaced by the new "everyone for himself" philosophy that's uncontrolled not only in the U.S.A. but also in the whole world. This new system isn't something we should be waiting for in the future. It's being established right now!

Globalism

You may now ask the question, "Should we support or oppose this new global democratic system?" My answer is "Neither!" By "we," I mean born-again Christians. We're in the world but not of the world. We're pilgrims just passing through on our way to eternal glory! The Bible does not encourage us to support or oppose one system or the other. When we do, we begin to fight with "flesh and blood."

However, it's impossible for any of us to exist without the new global democratic system. We're all part of it, whether we like it or not. Someone recently said, "We're all in the same water up to our necks." How true that is, but we'll not go under, because our destiny is in the Lord; we'll be going up in the Rapture!

To explain the new global democratic system, permit me to give an example. A reader wrote a letter complaining that in one of our magazine articles, I used kilometers, not miles, as a unit of measurement. The writer then correctly identified kilometers as the measurement of the global world system. "Why do you support it?" the reader asked.

This simple question showed that this person didn't really understand that we're living in a global society.

For example, if you buy a car, no matter what make, it's produced by a global corporation. The paper on which the

person wrote the letter probably was a global manufactur-
ing company. And so is the paper of this book.

When you shop at the local supermarket, you'll buy prod-
ucts produced primarily by global corporations. Can you
buy an airline ticket, make reservations at a hotel, or use a
telephone without involving a global corporation? The
answer is "No!"

Interdependence
What would happen if, for example, Americans would can-
cel all trade relations with all nations and concern themselves only with the U.S.A.?

A sixth-grade student should be able to figure out quickly
that within a few months, a large percentage of our work
force would be laid off, the stock markets would crash, and
the greatest concern of the average American citizen would
be, "How can I get something to eat today?"

Countries which aren't part of the global democratic society, such as Cuba and North Vietnam, are in a state of
despair, poverty, and starvation.

Today, the global world is a reality. We depend one upon
another and are more interconnected than we may think!
Read the following article as added proof:

Group says foreign firms sparking job growth in U.S.
Foreign firms are creating jobs in the United States five times
faster than American-owned companies, according to a study
by an international trade association.

The Organization for International Investment, a
Washington trade association for 60 foreign firms with U.S.
operations, found the largest concentration of such jobs in
California. Nevada was the leading state in job growth from
these investments. Americans working for the subsidiaries of
foreign corporations increased from 2.03 million in 1980 to 4.9

million in 1995, the latest year for which statistics are available, the trade association said."

An article appearing in *The State*, dated April 23, 1998, p.B-9

This article doesn't mention that American firms as well are creating countless jobs in foreign countries.

Democratic Babylon
This last Gentile kingdom described in the Book of Daniel isn't a clear-cut system. That means you can't identify it in a precise manner geographically.

Why not? Because it's worldwide. Neither is it identified nationally because it's international. It's for that reason the Bible calls this last kingdom in Revelation 17:5 *"Mystery, Babylon the great."* The word "mystery" shows us the unusual *character* of the last beast, which isn't limited to a certain geographic area but rather, it is *"of the Earth."*

I'm fully aware that it's difficult to call our beloved democratic system *"the abomination of the Earth."*

But, based on the Biblical analysis we've presented, there's no question in my mind that democracy is already ushering in the system of the Antichrist.

Whoever thinks that world peace will come when all nations implement democracy is correct, but only temporarily—they'll be dead wrong in the end.

Through democracy, the people of the Earth enjoy more freedom, liberty and prosperity than under any previous system of human government. However, that shouldn't lead us to believe that somehow democracy will usher in the kingdom of God.

A Voice From the 19th century
In the 19th century, Samuel Andrews wrote the following under the heading, "The Pantheistic Revolution":

"The multitude is made familiar with its principles through magazines and newspapers, through lectures and the pulpit. Its
prevalence is shown in the rapidity with which such systems as _Hitler &_
those of Christian Science, Mental Science, Theosophy, and _New Age_
others kindred to them, have spread in Christian communities,
for all have an atheistic basis. The moral atmosphere is full of
its spirit, and many are affected by it unawares. What shall we
say of its diffusion eventually?

To judge of this we must look upon its spread from another
point of view and consider its affinity with democracy."

—Samuel Andrews. *Christianity and Anti-Christianity In Their Final
Conflict.* Moody Press, Chicago. 1898. p.254

Even before communism and Nazism became a visible reality, Samuel Andrews recognized the beginning of Mystery
Babylon. He then continues:

"It is not to be questioned that social and political conditions
have much influence in molding religious opinions, and we
assume that the democratic spirit will rule the future. What
type of religious influence is democracy adapted to exert? In
what direction does the democratic current run?

"According to DeTocqueville, it runs in the direction of
very general ideas, and therefore to pantheism.

"The idea of the unity of the people as a whole, as one, pre-
ponderates, and this extends itself to the world, and to the universe. God and the universe make one whole. This unity has
charms for men living in democracies and prepares them for
pantheistic beliefs."

Today, there's little denying that the world is becoming one,
although before 1898, when Andrews wrote this, there was
no visible proof of such a coming world unity. Note also
that he pointed out the element of deception:

"Among the different systems, by whose aid philosophy tries to explain the universe, I believe pantheism to be one of those most fitted to seduce the human mind in democratic ages; and against it all who abide in their attachment to the true greatness of man, should struggle and combine.

"If these remarks of this very acute political observer are true, we may expect to see pantheism enlarging its influence in Christendom as democracy extends."

For the first time in world history, we've seen a united world in opposition to one country: Iraq. The U.N. enjoyed its first undisputed success, and will succeed in democratically and progressively enforcing (dictating) its laws over the behavior and policy of separate countries.

It's of interest that the United Nations resolution condemning Iraq was numbered 665, one short of 666.

Unceasingly, we're moving to the fulfillment of Bible prophecy, climaxing in the rulership of the Antichrist, whose number is 666!

Recognizing God's Way

Let me repeat: We must look beyond what we hear, see, and read in our news media. Otherwise, we're limiting ourselves to the symptoms and results of these world-shaking events, and we'll fail to understand the big picture, or to say it Biblically, the ways of God.

Let me give you an example: When the Israelites came out of Egypt through the power of God, they experienced mighty miracles. They saw the work of God as the water parted and they went through on dry ground. They also witnessed how the water destroyed the Egyptians. They were part of many miracles as they made their pilgrimage through the desert to the Promised Land. But the people only understood what they saw with their eyes and heard with their ears. There was only one exception: Moses saw the scene through God's eyes. We read later how the Psalmist proclaims the difference, *"He made known his ways unto Moses, his acts unto the children of Israel"* (Psalm 103:7).

If we only consider what the news media reports to us without realizing that God stands behind it all, and that He'll fulfill His prophetic Word, then we fail to receive God's wisdom, which He gladly gives to His children, according to James 1:5, *"If any of you lack wisdom, let him ask of God, that giveth to all men liberally, and upbraideth not; and it shall be given him."*

Babylon or Mystery Babylon?
Babylon (Iraq) has been highlighted in the global press for several decades now. But, as we've seen, the real goal is the establishment of Mystery Babylon.

Let's take a closer look at this "Mystery Babylon," therefore, so we will recognize how this last mysterious world empire will be organized. Today, the basic thing for the world is money, which translates into materialism. Money is success, and you can't argue success.

When Mystery Babylon finally finds her end, we read that those who mourn and weep for her are the ones who made the money, *"For all nations have drunk of the wine of the wrath of her fornication, and the kings of the Earth have committed fornication with her, and the merchants of the Earth are waxed rich through the abundance of her delicacies"* (Revelation 18:3).

Please note carefully that it says "all nations." Also, "the merchants of the Earth" grew rich through this political religious system, which the Bible condemns as "fornication." The descriptions are very negative: "drunk"; "wrath"; and "fornication." But the results are brighter, more positive words such as "rich," "abundance" and "delicacies."

If all nations take part in this prosperity, then we can expect an economic boom worldwide. Again, this is the big picture.

Religion is a Must

During the last fifty years or so, the free world, and more particularly, the Christian world, has taken much pain to identify *communism* as the evil system that threatened to lead to the Antichrist and world rulership.

We've always distanced ourselves from this interpretation because the final world empire will be extremely religious. Communism condemned religions with the statement, "Religion is the opiate of the people" or the much-popularized slogan, "God is dead."

We can describe communism as being anti-God. They opposed not only Christians, but also liberal churches including Jehovah Witnesses, Mormons, and other cults. Even the Muslims were experiencing oppression during communist rule. In stark contrast to that, we must understand one thing clearly: The last world empire will be *deeply religious* and this *religion* will be *mixed* with politics and economy. When we begin to understand that religion must experience a worldwide revival, then we can better understand why the Bible calls it "fornication": *"...the kings of the earth have committed fornication...."*

Christendom, or to be more precise, "churchianity," is strengthening ties with Islam, Buddhism, Hinduism, and many other religions the world over. Therefore, we must focus our attention on the system which successfully unites religion with prosperity.

Success and Failure

Meanwhile, during the process of the Earth becoming rich, there have been pitfalls, recessions, bankruptcy and new beginnings. In recent times, we've seen great financial and economic turmoil in Asia. When we observe this from the international platform, we quickly realize that this was to be expected because the Asian nations have been progressing too fast. The adjustment had to come. It's been painful, but normal. As far as the United States is concerned, her financial strength has been far undervalued. Thus, we've seen how the U.S. dollar has gained tremendous strength in comparison with most of the world's currencies.

Europe, the leader of the world, has also experienced a readjustment period, resulting in unemployment and budget deficits. At the time I write this, I see Europe recovering, taking on speed, and building a united super economy, based on a new currency, the euro.

One reason for Europe's economic slowdown was the fall of the Iron Curtain. The climax, no doubt, was the dismantling of the Berlin Wall. Europe's most powerful nation virtually bought a whole country (East Germany) for cash.

It may be of interest that Germany, East and West, united on October 3rd, 1990. They added 144 governing representatives of East Germany to the already existing 522 West German representatives to the Bundestag (Parliament). Adding the two makes 666! The cost of buying East Germany was phenomenal, and the readjustment took longer than originally expected. But the future is very bright.

Now, for the first time, all the former communist world can become a potential market for Europe. Some have estimated that by the year 2010, Europe will have solidified forty countries with a combined population of 800 million!

Global Babylon
How does this relate to Iraq (Babylon)? Answer: It shows that the new world empire, Mystery Babylon, is truly world-

wide. While the Gulf Conflict was authorized by the United Nations and the main force was supplied by the United States, the bill was paid primarily by Europe and Japan.

We must not overlook the important fact that the whole world is connected to the Middle East. The Gulf Conflict has clearly shown that it's impossible for a separate sovereign nation to act independently. No nation can operate fully independently of the democratic opinions of the world. This assembling of Mystery Babylon is in full progression today. Europe is becoming one, and with it the most powerful and richest bloc of nations are beginning to lead the world into unity, exactly as prophesied in Revelation 17:13, *"These have one mind, and shall give their power and strength unto the Beast."*

Israel and Global Babylon

Today, Israel, the little nation which is the key to all the conflicts of the world, and also the key to real world peace, is being overlooked during the formation of global Babylon. As the world power structures are fighting for their own turf, whether with weapons, oil, money, or politics, Israel is making tremendous progress.

Presently, Israel's hope is to be accepted into the European Union some day. This would guarantee her existence politically and economically, but that will lead Israel into the greatest danger ever, climaxing in the Great Tribulation.

When Mystery Babylon has reached the climax of her success, with the world united, peace and prosperity prevailing, then no other opinion will be tolerated. When the one-way united world democracy rules, then the time will come for Satan to give power to one person: the Antichrist. His aim will be to become God, to be worshipped, because he'll claim credit for the success of the New World Order.

It will be at that point Israel will finally perceive this deception and will oppose him. Then the Great Tribulation will start. It will no longer be communist against capitalist or the East against the West, but the whole world against Israel!

When the Prophet Jeremiah speaks of Babylon, and with it Mystery Babylon, he utters these words of grace and forgiveness, *"For Israel hath not been forsaken, nor Judah of his God, of the LORD of hosts; though their land was filled with sin against the Holy One of Israel"* (Jeremiah 51:5).

Yes, Israel will experience terrible tribulation and great oppression, but praise God, Israel won't be destroyed.

The death of her self-made success will be a new beginning. The same Prophet Jeremiah proclaims, *"Alas! for that day is great, so that none is like it: it is even the time of Jacob's trouble; but he shall be saved out of it"* (Jeremiah 30:7).

Jews kept their identity through
the Word of God.

Greek influence over the Western World
remains to this day.

Greek–Roman democracy is the foundation of the government of the United States.

Rome ruled when Jesus was born, and Rome will rule when He comes again!

Unity at all costs is the driving force behind the New World Order.

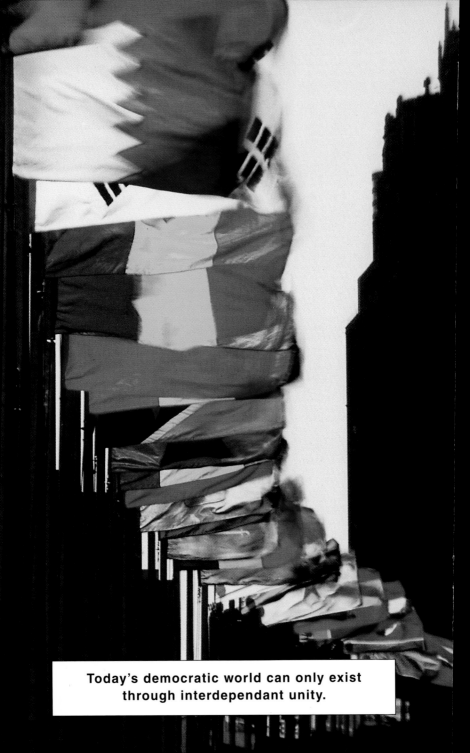

Today's democratic world can only exist through interdependant unity.

The Gulf War pitted ancient Babylon (Iraq) against "Mystery Babylon" (New World Order).

Arab oil: the power of unity.

Saddam Hussein has rebuilt the Ishtar Gate as a memorial to ancient Babylon.

**Pharoah's decision to eliminate Israel
caused his own demise!**

National borders marked with the European Union flag: twelve stars in a circle on blue.

Roman architecture:
Still alive after two millenia!

As in ancient Rome, the New World Order must accommodate all religions.

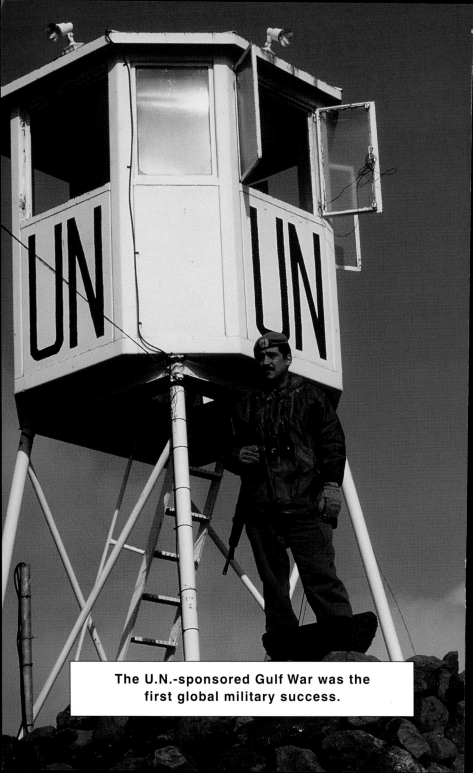

The U.N.-sponsored Gulf War was the first global military success.

Roman liberty, based on conquest and democracy, has shaped the Western World.

The Jews are God's chosen people. That's why every attempt to exterminate them has failed.

CHAPTER EIGHT

Saddam: Hoping To Build The New Babylon

—by James Rizzuti

James Rizzuti is the Associate Editor of *Midnight Call* and *News From Israel* magazines.

Summary

When the Gulf War started, people unfamiliar with the Bible asked, "Will this lead to Armageddon?" This chapter puts Saddam Hussein, today's Iraq, and the ancient kingdom of Nebuchadnezzar's Babylon into perspective. We see how political instability in the Middle East will be met with overwhelming global forces under the leadership of a man the Bible calls the "Antichrist."

Views on Saddam Hussein and the Gulf War:

"It was difficult to conceive, I think, in Washington, that this kind of irrationality [by Saddam Hussein] could in fact carry one on into a war."

—Rick Atkinson in *Crusade: The Untold Story of the Persian Gulf War*

"It's not at all clear what to do about a paranoid despot with biological and chemical weapons...In Saddam's world, he is the state, and Iraqis can be sacrificed for his survival."

—*Newsweek*, 3/2/98, p.32; 38

"Huddled in an underground bunker with his country smoldering in ruins around him, Iraqi President Saddam Hussein seemed buried for good in February, 1992.

"U.N. forces had devastated Iraq in the six-week Persian Gulf War; sewage systems and telephone lines were out, electrical grids were down, and roads were impassable.

"Harsh international sanctions and reparation debts hobbled recovery prospects for the oil-rich republic of Iraq. But Hussein resurfaced, unrepentant for the failed invasion of Kuwait and its enormous toll."

"'You Americans, you treat the Third World in the way an Iraqi peasant treats his new bride. Three days of honeymoon, and then it's off to the fields.'"

—Saddam Hussein, 1985 meeting with U.S. State Department officials[1]

"...most astute observers agree that the divide between radical Islam and the industrial democracies of the West has become the most destabilizing factor in world affairs."[2]

The war journal of a young Iraqi lieutenant, discovered in an abandoned base in Kuwait after the Iraqi soldiers left at the end of the Gulf War in 1991, testifies to the poor morale and terror experienced by the troops:

"I went to the…brigade at the bunker to move them to another place because of the raids and heavy bombing at the emplacement. When I got there, I found four bombs.

The situation was very difficult, because we had to pass close by them. But God protects. What an awful sight: One of the soldiers (disturbed) one of the bombs and suddenly it exploded and the soldier disappeared and I saw (two pieces) of his flesh on the second story of the bunker. Allah aqbar! [Arabic for "God is great."] What a horrible thing to see!"

"2 February, 1991—I was awakened this morning by the noise of an enemy air raid. I ran and hid in the nearby trench. I had breakfast and afterwards something indescribable happened.

"Two enemy planes came toward us and began firing at us, in turn, with missiles, machine guns and rockets. I was almost killed. Death was a yard away from me.

"The missiles, machine guns and rockets didn't let up. One of the rockets hit and pierced our shelter, which was penetrated by shrapnel.

"Over and over we said, 'Allah! Allah! Allah!'

"One tank burned and three other tanks belonging to 3rd Company, which we were with, were destroyed. That was a very bad experience.

"Time passed and we waited to die. The munitions dump of the 68th Tank Battalion exploded.

"A cannon shell fell on one of the soldiers' positions, but, thank God, no one was there. The soldiers were somewhere else. The attack lasted about 15 minutes, but it seemed like a year to me.

"I read chapters in the Qur'an [the Islamic Holy Book]. How hard it is to be killed by someone you don't know, you've never seen and can't confront. He is in the sky and you're on the ground.

"12 February, 1991—This morning, I learned that 26 soldiers from our division were condemned to death for deserting the front. They were apprehended near Samawa and executed at 2nd Division headquarters. Two of them were from the 68th Tank Battalion that we were with."[3]

New Weapons For a New World Order

From all of the sources I've reviewed as background to writing this chapter, this is one of the prominent points: The Gulf War demonstrated an entirely new class of military weaponry. High-tech has been brought to the killing field. This Iraqi soldier's journal recorded terror that must have been experienced thousands of times throughout the war.

Iraq, prior to its devastating war with Iran from 1980–88, had the 4th largest military force in the world, an estimated one-million-man army. Yet, the numbers are no match for the new devastating weapons that render troop numbers much more insignificant.

Stopping short of nuclear weapons, which carry such an enormous political and moral implication, and the very real danger of ultimate escalation of the conflict, generals and political leaders now have massive and unprecedented destructive options barely dreamed of before. Without launching nuclear weapons, they can order quick death on a massive scale.

Since technology is increasingly the determining factor in war, it will be difficult for a rogue nation to mount a credible and durable threat to the world. Options will be mainly limited to terrorism, however serious it may become. But there are other methods of dealing with that.

In awe, the entire world watched the essentially first tele-vised war, the Gulf War of 1991. Videotapes were displayed showing American fighter pilots using lasers to guide bombs to their targets. Viewers were assured that pilots had the ability to put their missiles through a window if need be, but that may have been an exaggeration since we were only repeatedly shown the same footage, displaying a laser-guided bomb hitting a target in a bullseye fashion. I would like to point out to our readers that the progressive destruc-tive power of these weapons is strongly hinted at in the Bible, where Jesus warned,

"For then shall be Great Tribulation, such as was not since the beginning of the world to this time, no, nor ever shall be. And except those days should be shortened, there should no flesh be saved: but for the elect's sake those days shall be shortened" (Matthew 24:21–22). Without His intervention, Jesus said, no one would survive the coming destruction in the Tribulation. We really began to see the reality of these kinds of weapons in the Gulf War.

The World Against One Man—Saddam Hussein
The U.S-led Allied war against Saddam Hussein followed a time when American foreign policy makers weren't even taking him seriously:

"...It's important to recognize that this development of Saddam's megalomania into a bellicosity which would lead him to invade Kuwait came at a time when the United States was completely preoccupied with the fall of the Berlin Wall which had happened in November of 1989, with the collapse of the Warsaw Pact, with the collapse of the Soviet Union. It's not as if Bush and Baker and the rest of the Bush Administration were not occupied with serious and important things. Saddam was a sideshow..."[4]

Essentially, the Gulf War started in opposition to the ambitions of this one man who has ruled Iraq with an iron fist since 1979.

While we can't answer all of the enigmas presented by him, we can trace the ambitions, the beliefs, the motivations and the chain of events that have placed him in such a pivotal role in these endtimes.

Biography—Learning to Kill at a Young Age

Saddam al-Tikriti Hussein was born April 28, 1937, in a small village in Tikrit, Iraq.

The young Saddam, whose first name roughly means "one who confronts," was raised by a devout Muslim nationalist uncle, Khayrallah Tulfah, an Iraqi army officer and crusader for Arab unity.

As a young boy, Saddam carried an iron rod to fend off attacks.

Reports indicate that he began killing at an early age. One arrest came when investigators found a sleeping Saddam, and a warm gun under his pillow. He had committed his first murder, that of a shepherd, while in his teens.

Baath Party Politics and Saddam's Violent Path

Saddam joined the socialist Baath Party when he was 19. Three years later, in 1959, a botched assassination attempt against Iraqi Prime Minister Abdul Karim Kassim left Saddam with a bullet in his leg, but he escaped and lived in Syria and Egypt from 1959–1963.[5]

The name "Baath" means "The Arab Renaissance Movement." The Baathist slogan is "One Arab nation, one immortal message!"

Right at the outset, we can begin to understand that Saddam Hussein's motivations are rooted in Baath Party politics.

The Baath Party has three important ideological linch-pins: 1) pan-Arab nationalism; 2) a distrust of the West; and 3) an unremitting desire to annihilate Israel. It would be fair to say that Saddam seems to be acting on these three main ideologies.

In 1968, he helped lead the revolt that finally brought the Baath Party to power under General Ahmed Hassan Bakr. In the process, he became vice president, and built a network of secret police to eliminate dissidents and rivals. Eleven years later, he deposed Bakr.

Saddam's years as a revolutionary taught him one sure method: Shortly after taking office as president, he purged 70 government officials suspected of "disloyalty." These actions have helped to earn him the title of "Butcher of Baghdad."

Saddam's ambition extends well beyond his country's borders. He envisions himself dominating the Muslim world.

How the Baath Party in Iraq Climbed to Power

Without oversimplifying the matter, the Baath Party as a reactionary force in Arab politics probably has a large part of its genesis in British policy early in this century.

During World War One, the Turkish Ottoman Empire, which controlled the area of Iraq, was defeated and the British ended up bossing the Middle Eastern deserts of old Babylon.

The vast wastelands had changed little over the centuries since the days of the Arab warriors. But the discovery and exploitation of oil changed all that. Western technology, money, and control began pouring in. But the oil money was flowing out of Iraq and that created massive discontent.

Britain drew the boundaries that defined Iraq and Kuwait in 1921, and in 1932, Iraq became independent.

The British installed a royal Arab dynasty: the Faisal family. But discontent led to an overthrow of Faisal, and American soldiers in the late 50's were called to the Gulf to protect American oil interests.

In 1961, the British were called upon to defend Kuwait when Iraq threatened to attack her tiny neighbor. Kuwait had been part of Iraq when the area was controlled by the Turkish Ottoman Empire, but Kuwait was split off by Britain in 1921 when Iraqi borders were drawn.

As in Africa, borders drawn by outsiders became the seeds of, or the excuses for, conflict later.

Leaders such as Saddam Hussein, with independent visions, seize these "injustices" as opportunities to launch attacks to regain "stolen" territory. That was precisely Saddam Hussein's excuse for invading Kuwait, but his real reasons are actually much deeper than that. Iraq's economy was in trouble, partially because of excessive military spending during a devastating eight-year war with Iran, and a reversal in the world market prices for crude oil.

The only solution for Saddam seemed to be control of more oil and higher prices. To Saddam's way of thinking, in a page straight out of a Muslim desert chieftain's handbook, conquering Kuwait was the easiest route to accomplish those goals. It certainly seemed easier than defeating Iran over the Shatt-al-Arab Waterway.

Hussein had wanted the territory on the Iranian side of the waterway, not only because he claimed it was Arabian and not Persian, but also because it was oil-rich. All of this was despite the fact that his country sits over some of the world's largest oil reserves. President Hussein expected citizens to bring in gold jewelry and gems to help pay for his war effort against Iran. This kind of intra-Middle East conflict can be traced back to the days of the rival caliphs and desert tribal bosses who struggled over camels and women.

But, today, the stakes are much higher because they threaten to envelop the entire world due to the oil.

For centuries, the desert sands of what is now called Iraq remained largely untouched, and agricultural methods changed little since Bible times. But the discovery of oil changed all that.

A Bloody Pathway to Power

Saddam officially become president in 1979, emphasizing his position across Iraq through giant 20-foot-tall posters.

In 1980, shortly after becoming president and finally obtaining the long-sought-after ability to regain "Iraqi territory," Hussein ordered the invasion of Iran, triggering eight years of carnage that analysts estimate cost one million people their lives, with millions of others injured or somehow permanently scarred.

The regime's talk focused on martyrs and a noble cause, while stalemate was painted over with the insistence that it was a glorious victory.

Both sides in the Iraq-Iran war resorted to long-range rocket attacks on civilian population centers.

Pages remain to be written in this new and ugly chapter in the history of Persia and Babylon (Iran and Iraq) which really began with the religious ascent of Ayatollah Ruhollah Khomeini in Iran. He led the fundamentalist Islamic revolution in the 70's that extracted the Western-allied Shah of Iran from power and reignited the ancient rivalry between Arab and Persian power.

The Western powers, wary of Iran's fundamentalist fever, were silently happy to see the two powers neutralizing each other.

Actually, Iraq has no real friends in the international community. Moderate trade with Jordan takes place, but otherwise, Saddam's Iraq is a loner in the Arab desert.

In 1990, Hussein sent his army into Kuwait, seizing the entire country in just 12 hours. He called it Iraq's "19th province." The literature is replete with atrocities committed by Hussein's troops—however, some of the highly publicized events were later found to be "Allied propaganda." The brutality was intended to frighten the Kuwaitis into submission. Nevertheless, in building his case against Saddam, George Bush called him "Hitler revisited."

Here's how *Newsweek* put it:

"Saddam's resumé ranks him among the most brutal of dictators. This is a man who, upon taking power, calmly sucked on a cigar at a party convention as he sent 22 of his closest associates off for execution. A man who, according to Western intelligence reports, has pulled out a pistol during meetings, executed generals who disagreed with him and then proceeded with his agenda."[6]

In addition to his numerous executions of rivals and those he perceived as questioning his authority, Saddam once imprisoned his own son, Uday, on a murder charge. But before you feel sorry for Uday, read what *Newsweek* had to say about him:

"Saddam's son is given to violent rages. He once ordered the Iraqi national football team beaten on the soles of their feet after a loss in the World Cup tournament. Imagine what he could do with a stock of chemical and biological weapons."[7]

Writing on the subject of the dangers of Arab regimes obtaining weapons of mass destruction, Hal Lindsey writes,

"More than anytime since the Crusades, Islam is posing a serious threat to the Western World. It now possesses the wealth and the modern lethal weaponry to supplant the Soviet Union as the greatest challenge to the Judeo-Christian-based Western world order."[8]

One reason Western analysts are cautious about Saddam is his willingness to use chemical warfare.

He used chemical weapons against Iran, and to quell a Kurdish uprising in his own country. His army lobbed chemicals into a Kurdish village, slaughtering women and children in one of the most horrifying genocidal scenes in recent memory. Those were scenes that really turned the world against him. Following the horrors of World War I, the nations of the world decided they wanted no more of that kind of warfare, and passed resolutions against it. But, of course, all bets are off in war.

The Mystique of Saddam Hussein
Commenting on his reputation, Hussein once said,

> "Weakness doesn't assure achieving the objectives required by a leader."

Apparently, this is a conviction shared by a large majority of the 22 million people living in Iraq, 75 to 80% of whom are Arab, 15 to 20% of whom are Kurdish.

Despite the well-documented dark nature of Saddam Hussein, he is revered with fanaticism by his people, who apparently believe he is the one man who can unify the Arab nations against the West. A comprehensive video report on Hussein's life described it this way:

> "There are many stories of the young fanatic who literally fought his way up the party machine, personally murdering as

he established his credentials for command in what has always been a violent society."[9]

Saddam has been described as a recluse who is fanatical about security. As the U.N.-authorized Allies moved into position to launch air strikes against Iraq in 1998, and as Marines were unloading in Kuwait, media reports said that Hussein was moving around Baghdad in an old taxi cab and lodging overnight with Iraqi citizens:

"Each day in Iraq, bodyguards knock on the front doors of more than a half-dozen homes. Then they announce: 'You'll have a guest tonight.' They allow the startled residents a few minutes to pack toothbrushes and a change of clothes before heading off, sometimes to a room reserved in a luxury hotel. The families would be foolish to resist because their guest is Saddam Hussein, engaged in one of his many elaborate rituals to confuse potential assassins. Only as night falls does Iraq's president, a man with dozens of residences, choose a place to sleep."[10]

No doubt, he has taken a lesson from an incident involving Libyan strongman Muamar Khadaffi, whose personal tent was hit by U.S. jets on order of President Ronald Reagan, killing a daughter. After that incident, the Libyan caliph removed himself from the world radar screen.

Hussein has not traveled outside the Arab world since 1985, where he would be in constant mortal danger, possibly even finished off by Israel's Mossad.

A 1983 book published by his former intelligence chief states that Saddam survived seven assassination attempts in 15 years.

Today, he appears ever more determined to survive in order to trouble the world another day:

> "Human guinea pigs taste his food for poison; surgically altered doubles make public appearances; secretaries hand him photocopies of all his letters in case the originals are smeared with toxins. He travels in long convoys of Mercedes-Benz sedans, switching cars along the route."[11]

Despite the almost world-wide condemnations of his invasions and his rule by intimidation, he enjoys popularity among the average Arab for his pro-Palestinian, anti-Western and anti-Israeli views.

Saddam Hussein has also shown his tyrannical ways in his dealings with his own military. It has been reported that many of the commanders who survived his war with Iran were systematically purged and murdered to eliminate them as a political threat to his rule. And, after coup rumblings in 1997, he arrested and executed more than 100 military officers. Obviously, Saddam has lived through 20 coup attempts by trusting no one.

He has surrounded himself with a cabinet that supports his every move and, it is believed, shielded him from many of the facts regarding U.S. and Allied troop strength. At least that would explain his seemingly endless mistakes with regard to Western responses to his actions.

Actually, Saddam has never served in the Iraqi military and he has no official military training of any kind.

The Fatalistic Mindset

Hussein regards war with the United States and Israel as a "destiny" he must fulfill. He seemed eager to get involved in "the mother of all battles," with the U.S.-led Allies.

This is a fatalistic mindset shared by many Arab leaders. They will plunge ahead with plans that will devastate themselves and many other people, somehow thinking that 'destiny" or "Allah" will order the way, regardless.

Palestinian Authority President Yasser Arafat confesses to it. The actions of Gamel Abdel Nasser, ruler of Egypt in the 50's and 60's, his successor, Anwar Sadat, and Syrian President Hafez al-Asad also seem to fit the mold.

This inclination toward delusional thinking has been clearly portrayed in a video detailing Hussein's path to power. After the catastrophic Iran-Iraq war that Saddam initiated, the cease-fire was presented to the Iraqi public as glorious victory.

Saddam took to a white horse and clopped down the streets of Baghdad, exultant, triumphant, and proud.[12]

Lavish and sprawling memorials to the war dead were built. Ninety-nine statues representing his fallen commanders were set up along the Shatt-al-Arab Waterway pointing accusing fingers at Iran. But it had been Saddam who had started the war!

Iran and Iraq restored diplomatic relations in 1990. They are negotiating agreements settling outstanding disputes from their eight-year war concerning border demarcation, prisoners-of-war, freedom of navigation and sovereignty over the Shatt al Arab Waterway.

In November 1994, Iraq accepted the U.N.-determined border with Kuwait, which had been spelled out in Security Council Resolutions #687 (1991), #773 (1993), and #883 (1993). That formally ended earlier claims to Kuwait and the struggle over water development plans by Turkey for the Tigris and Euphrates Rivers.[13]

Current Issues for Iraqi Concern

Government water control projects have drained most of the inhabited marsh areas by drying up or diverting the feeder streams and rivers. Furthermore, the destruction of the natural habitat poses serious threats to the area's wildlife populations.

A once sizable population of Shi'a Muslims, who have inhabited these areas for thousands of years, has been displaced, which feeds political unrest.

The problem of inadequate supplies of potable water for the fast-growing population must be addressed, especially for a fast-growing population, and development of the Tigris-Euphrates river systems are contingent upon agreements with Turkey. Air and water pollution, soil degradation (salinization) and erosion, desertification, and natural hazards remain of more than average concern.[14]

The Aspiring Nebuchadnezzar Leading the Arab World to Global Power?

Some real contradictions in the Arab world make analysts question whether Arab society as a whole is really ready to enter the modern world. Despite decades of incredible income from oil, vast teeming masses live in desperate poverty.

Kuwait's "Empty Apartment Syndrome"

I'll never forget the conversation I once had with a Lebanese Muslim, who formerly lived in Kuwait and who owned and operated a Subway restaurant. At the time, in the mid-80's, I was living in Myrtle Beach, South Carolina, and working as a television news director.

This Muslim man related how the government of Kuwait had spent a lot of money building modern apartment buildings in the desert to house its citizens.

But, the apartment buildings remained mostly empty because the people simply preferred living in tents in the desert, just like they had for centuries! Many Arabs, living out their Bedouin culture, simply did not want to have anything to do with modern Western-style conveniences. They only came for medical help when they were sick.

The Future of the Arab World

No doubt, Arab countries will modernize, but it will not be a quick process. When the oil begins to be depleted, they will be in critical difficulty, as they have not established any significant alternative economic base to support their people. It is unfortunate, but true, that Arab nations have made few contributions to the modern civilized world. When was the last time you bought anything, other than oil, that originated from an Arab country?

Nevertheless, many analysts have noted Saddam Hussein's preoccupation with becoming the new "Nebuchadnezzar" who will finally lead "the unified Arab nation" to its rightful place at the head of the world.

That certainly is a totally deluded idea. But he is not the only one who sees big things ahead for the Arab world. Muslim proponents are expounding their belief that the next century will be "the century of Islam." They certainly have money from oil. Author Grant Jeffrey writes,

> "...the Iraqi government has already spent over $600 million in rebuilding a large number of Temples, palaces and amphitheaters to honor the pagan gods of ancient Babylon.
>
> "Every summer, a Babylonian Festival is held with over 4,000 invited guests from around the world to witness the most unique rebuilding project in history."[15]

In this regard, it must be admitted that Saddam has aimed as high as possible in seeking to link his name with that of Nebuchadnezzar, the greatest of all kings on Earth at that time— in the sixth century, B.C. During his reign of 45 years, the bulk of the Babylonian empire was built, extending his power throughout most of the then-known world. Nebuchadnezzar's colossal city of Babylon, with dimensions and building specifications that are almost impossible to believe (60 miles around; walls 80 feet thick and 300 feet high, extending 35 feet below ground), was situated in the cradle of human civilization around the Tower of Babel.

The SIZE and Specifications of Babylon

According to *Halley's Bible Handbook*, there was 1/4-mile of clear space between the city and the wall all the way around. The wall was protected by wide and deep moats (canals) filled with water. There were 250 towers on the wall, guard rooms for soldiers, and 100 gates made of brass.

The city was divided by the Euphrates into two almost equal parts. Both banks were guarded by brick walls all the way, with 25 gates connecting streets, and ferry boats. One bridge on stone piers was 1/2-mile long and 30 feet wide, featuring drawbridges which were removed at night. A tunnel under the river was 15 feet wide and 12 feet high.

The Great Temple of Marduk, adjoining the Tower of Babylon, was the most renowned sanctuary in all the Euphrates Valley. It contained a golden image of Bel [Bel—the national god of the Babylonians] and a golden table which together weighed not less than 50,000 pounds.

At the top were golden images of Bel and Ishtar [the Babylonian fertility goddess], two golden lions, a golden table 40 feet long and 15 feet wide, and a human figure of solid gold 18 feet high.

Truly, Babylon was a "city of gold," (Isaiah 14:4), and very religious: It included 53 Temples, and 180 altars to Ishtar.

It may have been in the place between the Tower of Babylon and the palace of Nebuchadnezzar that the "image of gold" described in Daniel 3:1 was set up.

The "Hanging Gardens" of Babylon were one of the Seven Wonders of the ancient world, built by Nebuchadnezzar for his Median queen.

Babylonian Religious Roots in Idolatry

Most people are shocked when they finally realize the size, scope, and greatness of the Babylonian empire, led at the height of its glory by Nebuchadnezzar.

In Daniel's day, the city of Babylon was not only the world's greatest city, but ruled the most powerful empire that had ever been built, an empire that lasted for 70 years.

Excavations of recent years have, to a large extent, verified the seemingly fabulous accounts of ancient historians.[16]

But what about the actual religion that inflamed Babylon's residents and was a large part of the success of building this empire? What was *it* all about? *Halley's Bible Handbook* gives us significant clues:

"Abraham was not an idolater. But he lived in a world of idolatry. In the beginning, man had ONE God; and, in the Garden of Eden, had lived in rather intimate Communion with God. But, with Adam's sin and [subsequent] banishment, man lost his primeval knowledge of God; and, groping in his darkness for a solution of the mysteries of existence, he came to worship the powers of Nature which seemed to him to be the sources of life.

"Sex, because it was the means through which life came, played a very important part in early Babylonian religion. Cuneiform inscriptions have revealed that a large part of their liturgies were descriptions of sexual intercourse between gods and goddesses, through which, they thought, all things came into being.

"Then, too, the sun and rain and various forces of nature were deified, because on them depended the life of the world.

"And kings also, because they had power, came to be deified.

"Many cities and nations had for their chief god their founder. Asshur, father of the Assyrians, became the chief god

Wilderness of Sin - in Arabia

of the Assyrians. Marduk (Nimrod), father of Babylon, became chief god of Babylon.

"And, to make their gods more real, images were made to represent the gods and then the images themselves came to be worshiped as gods.

"Thus, man took his nosedive from original monotheism into the abyss of innumerable polytheistic... cultures, some of which, in their practices, were unspeakably vile and abominable...

"Ur was in Babylonia; and Babylonians had many gods and goddesses. They were worshippers of fire, the sun, moon, stars and various forces of nature.

"Nimrod, who had exalted himself against God in building the Tower of Babel, was ever afterward recognized as the chief Babylonian deity. Marduk was the common form of his name, later becoming identical with Bel.

"Shamash was the name of the sun god.

"Sin, the moon god, was the principal deity of Ur, Abraham's city. [When the Bible mentions 'the wilderness of sin,' it is not talking about the 'wilderness of wrongdoing,' it is a reference to the name of an Egyptian town and adjoining desert—the wilderness of the moon god in Arabia.]

"Sin's wife was called Ningal, the moon goddess of Ur. She had many names, and was worshiped in every city as the mother goddess. Nina was one of her names, from which the city of Nineveh was named. Her commonest name in Babylonia was Ishtar."[17]

There is no mystery about this. The licentiousness of the Ishtar religion stemmed from Nimrod's mother, Semiramis. From the Biblical perspective, she is a perfect example of a vile woman: rebellious, loud, dominant, and covered with gaudy jewelry. Semiramis is, at the same time, the model for today's pagan woman and for that reason, it is no surprise that Babylonian goddess worship is making a comeback world-wide today.

Nebuchadnezzar's Greatness
Scripture buttresses the temporal greatness of Nebuchadnezzar.

When listing the four gentile world empires that would come to pass, the Bible refers to Nebuchadnezzar as the best, the "head of gold" in Daniel 2:37–38, *"Thou, O king [Nebuchadnezzar], art a King of kings: for the God of heaven hath given thee a kingdom, power, and strength, and glory.*

"And wheresoever the children of men dwell, the Beasts of the field and the fowls of the heaven hath he given into thine hand, and hath made thee ruler over them all. Thou art this head of gold."

How the Bible Pictures Nebuchadnezzar
The Bible indicates that four great Gentile empires would succeed each other in the government of the world, from Nebuchadnezzar to the Second Coming of Christ: the Babylonian (gold, led by Nebuchadnezzar), Medo-Persian (silver, led by Darius), Grecian (brass, led by Alexander the Great), and Roman (iron, led by the caesars).

The empires are represented by a huge statue of a man made out of components that progressively become less valuable: from gold to silver, then brass, followed by iron, and finally iron and clay.

"But the "Colossus" grows weaker and weaker until the feet and toes become a mixture of iron and clay.

"In other words, the government degenerates from an absolute monarchy to an autocratic democracy, a form of government in which the people largely have the say."[18]

Ironically, the original Babylonians, the builders of the Tower of Babel, were democratically minded:

"And they said, Go to, let us build us a city and a tower, whose top may reach unto heaven; and let us make us a name, lest we be scattered abroad upon the face of the whole Earth.

"And the LORD came down to see the city and the tower, which the children of men builded.

"And the LORD said, Behold, the people is one [in democratic unity], and they have all one language; and this they begin to do: and now nothing will be restrained from them, which they have imagined to do." [19]

We hasten to remind you that Adolf Hitler and Saddam Hussein both received nearly unanimous democratic support from their subjects. Democracy is certainly no guarantee of humanity or decency in government.

Some Archaeological/Historical Notes

The confusion of tongues at the Tower of Babel occurred in the 4th generation after the Flood of Noah and about 325 years before the call of Abraham. *Halley's Bible Handbook* gives us the following details:

"The traditional site of the Tower of Babel is at Borsippa, 10 miles southwest from the center of Babylon…It is commonly thought by archaeologists that more likely, the actual site was in the center of Babylon, identified with the ruins just north of the Marduk Temple. G. Smith found an ancient tablet reading:

'The building of this illustrious tower offended the gods. In a night, they threw down what they had built. They scattered them abroad, and made strange their speech.'

"This seems like a tradition of Babel. It is now an immense hole 330 feet square, which has been used as a quarry from which to take bricks. When standing, it consisted of a number of successive platforms, one on top of another, each smaller than the one below, a sanctuary to Marduk [Nimrod] on the top. ...Sir Henry Rawlinson, an archaeologist, found a cylinder [at Borsippa] with this inscription:

'The tower of Borsippa, which a former king erected, and completed to a height of 42 cubits, whose summit he did not finish, fell to ruins in ancient times....The great god Marduk urged me to restore it. I did not alter its site, or change its foundation walls. At a favorable time, I renewed its brick work and its roofing tiles, and I wrote my name on the cornices of the edifice. I built it anew as it had been ages before; I erected its pinnacle as it was in remote days.'

"This seems like a tradition of the unfinished Tower of Babel.

"In Genesis 11;4, '...a tower with its top in heaven' is an expression of the vast pride of the first builders of 'ziggurats,' the artificial Temple hills of Sumeria and Babylonia.

"The notion was to concentrate, to build powerful groups and cities instead of obeying the command of Genesis 9:1 to spread out. The old spirit of rebellion, the worship of man, and human pride was again in control.

"Ziggurats still exist in ruin at Ur and Erech and their construction illustrates Genesis 11:3–4. Their whole purpose...was idolatrous worship and herein lay the sin of the Babel builders." [20]

Hussein's Islam: For Public Consumption?

Although not regarded as a religious man, in recent times, Saddam has taken a more public profile in Islam and has called for a "jihad" (holy war) against the Allied forces. His pilgrimage to Mecca and televised scenes showing him lifting hands to "Allah"[21] in prayer have probably been for public consumption rather than expressions of true Islamic faith.

Like many leaders in the West, Hussein might only call on the Divine when things are going hopelessly bad for him in the political or military realm. The phrase ALLAHU AKBAR (God is Great) was added to the Iraqi flag in January, 1991 during the Persian Gulf crisis.

Nevertheless, Saddam appears ready and willing to exploit the religious justification for Islamic "jihad" in the Qur'an, the Muslim holy book which commands that "infidels," (non-believers in Islam) be killed, or at best, be forced into submissive tribute to Islamic overlords.

The Two Houses of Islam
While it is difficult to measure the degree of actual religious motivation of Saddam Hussein and his true adherence to Muslim religious teaching, there is no doubt whatsoever that he will exploit it whenever possible.

This translates into political policy that has "religious/moral authority" in the Arab world. It is obvious that the teeming Arab masses want an ultra-strong leader who will fearlessly blacken the eye of the West when any perceived Arab/Islamic interest or policy is challenged.

Meanwhile, the sentiment toward Israel, of course, is the desire for total annihilation.

Since these sentiments have Qur'anic and Hadithic religious foundation, they are held with impunity and resolute conviction. Terrorism or outright military destruction are viewed as Allah's perfect and holy will against the "infidel," that is, anyone who is not Muslim.

The religious accommodation in Islam, reserved for Jews and Christians as "people of the Book," is applicable only when those populations are willingly submissive to all Islamic dictates and humbly accept the status of "dhimmitude," paying heavy taxes as well. Any rebellion cancels the accommodation and is to be answered with the sword.

That is fundamental Islamic doctrine. Those of *other* religious persuasion, such as Hindus, Bahais, Buddhists, or whatever—they are simply to be exterminated when Islam takes over the territory in question. That, too, is fundamental Islamic doctrine. Westerners should understand that within Islam, there is no "separation of church and state." Islam rules in the affairs of Muslims across the entire spectrum of life, from food and clothing to politics and relationships between men and women. Everything.

The "House of Islam," according to Islamic teaching, is divided into two parts: Dar Al Islam and Dar Al Harb.

Dar Al Islam/Dar Al Harb

The "domain of the faithful," is "Dar Al Islam." That translates into the territory now occupied and governed under the Islamic religion. In the Muslim religion, once territory is conquered for "Allah," it is considered the eternal property of Islam, and war ("jihad") is always justified—in fact, commanded by the Qur'an—to gain it back.

That alone is one simple reason why Israel will never be granted "peace" by the Islamic hordes that surround her. She will only be granted peace through the miraculous intervention of the Antichrist, who will somehow temporarily tame the Islamic religious sentiment to destroy Israel.

In contrast to "Dar Al Islam," all other real estate on the globe is referred to as "Dar Al Harb," the "domain of those whom Islam is at war with until judgment day,"[22] which is the remainder of the world in which Islam is not the dominant religious and political philosophy. Thus, the ultimate goal of religious Islam, at least on paper, is the subjugation of the entire world, by the sword if necessary.

Most Western people have no idea that this is a central Muslim doctrine. But it cannot be passed off as the fuming of just a couple of wild-eyed fundamentalist mullahs.

The Father of Modern-Day Terrorism

The unquestioned spiritual father of modern-day fundamental Islam (and modern-day terrorism) is the now-dead
Iranian Ayatollah Ruhollah Khomeini. Here's how Islam's
leading spiritual authority put it:

> "The governments of the world should know that Islam cannot
> be defeated. Islam will be victorious in all the countries of the
> world, and Islam and the teachings of the Qur'an will prevail
> all over the world."[23]

Fundamental Muslims believe this to their bone marrow and
teach it. I will never forget watching the television coverage
of Khomeini's funeral. Huge masses of people appeared to
be almost going out of their minds with grief and emotion.

So revered was Khomeini that the hysterical mob
dumped his body out on the ground and ripped away pieces
of the dead man and his clothes, simply to get a part of the
man they believed would lead them to a global Islamic
resurgence.

The Actual Words of the "Prophet" Muhammad

Should you still be unsure about Islamic doctrine in this
matter of reconquering territory formerly occupied and controlled by Islam, and expanding into formerly non-Islamic
countries, let's look at the actual words of Muhammad:

> "Regarding offensive wars or imposing the Islamic religion on
> people by war, Muhammad said: 'I was commanded to fight
> people until they say, 'There is no God but the only God, and
> Muhammad is the apostle of God,' and they perform all the
> Islamic ordinances and rituals.''
>
> "We also examined Muhammad's attitude toward the apos-
> tate: He made it clear that the apostate must be sentenced to

death. He said about those who relinquish Islam: 'Whoever changes his faith...kill him!'"[24]

What An Islamic "Peace Agreement" Really Means

Truces and treaties, according to Islamic teaching, are tools to enable them to get into a better position to win the ultimate war. This was the war that Saddam Hussein apparently thought he was going to win. He called it the "mother of all battles."

It reminded me of the same bellicose and deluded statements of Egypt's Gamel Abdul Nasser prior to the 1967 Middle East War. Nasser bragged that he was "longing for the day to battle Israel." Well, Nasser got his long-sought-after opportunity, and was pounded into humiliating defeat in just a few days.

I think the point is well-made that Islam has no intention of remaining confined to "Dar-al-Islam." The objective is to conquer "Dar-al-harb," and the monster will only be tamed by the giant world political and religious democracy machine, the "Mystery Babylon" that Arno Froese has been telling us about. It underscores the power and influence that this new Mystery Babylon will have. It will be the only force capable of containing Islam.

Saddam Hussein's Mistakes: They Are Legion

"Here was a man who came to believe that the United States, first of all, would turn a blind eye to control of 40% of the world's oil supply.

"He was a man who believed that he could hunker down and ride out an attack by what was clearly the most formidable coalition of military powers since World War II.

"He was a man who believed that the West lacked a political will to carry through on its threats.

"He was a man who miscalculated in taking hostages and then compounded his miscalculations and made [U.S. General Normal] Schwarzkopf's military efforts much easier by letting them go...

"Every time he had to make a major strategic decision, Saddam guessed wrong...

"Saddam made many strategic miscalculations. He failed to recognize that the world was awash with oil; that Iraqi oil was not critical to the functioning of the Western democracies. There was plenty of oil.

"He failed to recognize that Arab unity would hold even in the face of attacks on Israel and the potential for Israel to come into the war.

"He failed to reassure King Fahd of his benign intentions toward Saudi Arabia; thereby, driving the Saudis into the arms of Washington.

"Perhaps most importantly, he failed to calculate that the United States was serious about this; that there had been a decision made in Washington that they would go to war.

"I think he believed that the United States would fold as it had after the bombing of the Marine barracks in Lebanon in 1983 and simply leave.

"He made one strategic miscalculation after another."[25]

The Facts On This Desert Dictatorship

The CIA has published a map showing basic facts about the nation of Iraq. This country is mostly useless desert. Only about 12% of the country is arable, along the Euphrates River mainly, an arm of the fertile crescent. But only 1% of the land is devoted to permanent crops.

Keep in mind that this area was once the center of God's creation in the Garden of Eden, the perfect picture of His provision. Under the dominance of the spirit of Babylon, it has become largely a useless ruin of baked sand.

It is a perfect Bible metaphor showing the contrast between good and evil.

Half of the population of this area is under 14 years of age, and from an early age, they are taught the god-myth of Saddam. Small children are dressed in mini army fatigues, preparing their minds to sacrifice their lives for Saddam, Iraq, and Allah. This flood of children seems sure to increase, as the average Iraqi woman bears 6.41 children, and the population increases approximately 3.69% per year!

Only about 58% of those 15 and over can read and write; only 45% of the women can do so.

Religiously, 97% of the people are Muslims, 60–65% of them are of the more radical and violent Shi'a sect, while only about 35% are the more moderate Sunni Muslims[26] [such as those in the majority in Saudi Arabia].

To put it succinctly, I would frame the distinction this way: The Sunni Muslims may believe in Allah, but they are not nearly as willing to die for him as the Shi'as are. These statistics that give us a picture of Iraqi culture are a formula for the continuance of dictatorship and religious fanaticism in Iraq. But, nevertheless, this nation will sooner or later have to come under the sway of Mystery Babylon, the religious/political democracy machine now sweeping the globe.

NOTES

1   *Los Angeles Times*, Feb. 10, 1991. (Cited by ABC News)

2   Lindsey, Hal. *The Final Battle*. Palos Verdes, California: Western Front, Ltd. 1995. p.46

3   An Iraqi lieutenant's journal from the historical text archive at Mississippi State University. http://www.msstate.edu/Archives/History/USA/GulfWarftp.msstate.edu/docs/history/USA/Gulf War

4   *The Gulf War*. PBS TV, 1996. WGBH Educational Foundation. Interview with Rick Atkinson, author of *Crusade:The Untold Story of the Persian Gulf War*.

5   *Saddam Hussein: Defying the World*. Independent Television News, 1990. Videotape.

6   "Saddam's Secret World" *Newsweek*, 3/2/98, p.39

7   "Thunder In the Desert" *Newsweek*, 3/2/98, p.37

8   Lindsey, Hal. *The Final Battle*. Palos Verdes, California: Western Front, Ltd. 1995. p.12

9   OP. CIT. *Saddam Hussein: Defying the World*.

10   "Saddam's Secret World." *Newsweek*, 3/2/98. p.38

11   IBID. p.38

12   OP. CIT. *Saddam Hussein: Defying the World*.

13   CIA World Fact Book (Internet page).

14   IBID.

15   Jeffrey, Grant. *Apocalypse: The Coming Judgment Of the Nations*. Frontier Research Publications, Toronto. 1992. p.171

16   Halley, Henry. *Halley's Bible Handbook*. Grand Rapids, Michigan: Zondervan Publishing House. 1965. p. 336–337, 340

17   Halley's Bible Handbook, p. 94–95

18   Larkin, Clarence. *Dispensational Truth or God's Plan and Purpose For the Ages*. Glenside, PA: Rev. Clarence Larkin Estate, 1920. p.67

19   Genesis 11:4–6 [emphasis within text is ours]

20   Halley's Bible Handbook, p. 83–84

21   "Allah" is the name of the Islamic god. The name derives from pagan pre-Islamic Arabia, where "Allah" was the moon god idol, the "chief idol" in the Kabah at Mecca, along with 360 other pagan idol gods.

22   Missler, Chuck. *Steeling the Mind of America*. Green Forest, Arkansas: New Leaf Press, p.185

23   Lindsey, Hal. *The Final Battle*. Palos Verdes, California: Western Front, Ltd. 1995. p.1

24   Author's name and publisher withheld for security reasons. *Behind the Veil*. p.72

25   OP. CIT. *The Gulf War*.

26   CIA World Fact Book (Internet page).

CHAPTER NINE

Jerusalem or Babylon?

—by Dr. Wim Malgo

Dr. Wim Malgo is the founder of Midnight Call Ministries. He went home to be with the Lord on August 8th, 1992. This chapter was published in April of 1968, and we deliberately present it to point out the accuracy with which Dr. Malgo analyzed events relating to Iraq and Babylon of antiquity.

Summary

The diversity and contradiction between the two cities becomes evident when we realize that Babylon has been erased, but Jerusalem still exists. Dr. Malgo maps the spiritual journey from the beginning to the end of the Gentile power. How believers in Christ should analyze the old Babylon to really benefit spiritually is the priority of this chapter.

In the third year of the reign of Jehoiakim king of Judah
came Nebuchadnezzar king of Babylon unto Jerusalem,
and besieged it.

*"And the Lord gave Jehoiakim king of Judah into his
hand, with part of the vessels of the house of God: which he
carried into the land of Shinar to the house of his god; and
he brought the vessels into the treasure house of his god"*
(Daniel 1:1–2).

The time of the Prophet Daniel is very similar to our time.
There was a world-wide change: The global rule which had
been given to the people of Israel was taken from them and
given to the Gentiles.

Israel was destined to rule the world, *"And all people of
the earth shall see that thou art called by the name of the
LORD; and they shall be afraid of thee*

*"And the LORD shall make thee the head, and not the
tail; and thou shalt be above only, and thou shalt not be
beneath..."* (Deuteronomy 28:10 and 13).

Genesis 49:10 also speaks of Israel's rule over the
nations, *"The sceptre shall not depart from Judah, nor a
lawgiver from between his feet, until Shiloh come; and unto
him shall the gathering of the people be."*

In God's eyes, Israel is the relevant nation in world history. But, she was unfaithful to the Lord and worshipped
idols. Then, Nebuchadnezzar, the first ruler of the Gentile
world empire, Babylon, came to Jerusalem. Daniel lived in
the time of the collision between Babylon and Jerusalem.

Today, we have a similar situation, but in reverse: the collision between Jerusalem and Babylon.

In Daniel's time, Babylon gained the upper hand and
overcame Jerusalem. What a terrible tragedy! The city of
the great King was ruled by the spirit of Babylon.

And today? Jerusalem defies world Babylon. God is
beginning to remove the Gentiles from world rulership,

although now, things seem to be going in the opposite direction. The political developments in our day will culminate however, in Jerusalem's rulership over the whole world when the great King, Jesus Christ, will come from heaven and ascend to His throne in that city.

This is the reason for the increasing rejection of Israel and world-wide anti-Semitism, just as described in Luke 21:24, *"And they shall fall by the edge of the sword, and shall be led away captive into all nations: and Jerusalem shall be trodden down of the Gentiles, until the times of the Gentiles be fulfilled."*

Meanwhile, since June 7th, 1967, Jerusalem hasn't been *"...trodden down of the Gentiles..."* but is in Israel's hands.

What Is Babylon? And How Does It Compare To Jerusalem?

First, Babylon represents all that's ungodly, the denial of the rulership of God.

There's also a Babylon, however, in the heart of man, which is expressed in disobedience and opposition to God.

It's the "I will" of man against the "I will" of God.

Second, Babylon represents the effort to fulfill self-redemption. The Babylonians said, *"...Let us build us a city and a tower, whose top may reach unto heaven..."* (Genesis 11:4).

And Nebuchadnezzar exclaimed, *"...Is not this great Babylon, that I have built...?"* (Daniel 4:30).

Babylon is religion without the cross; it's the rejection of the cross. But, Jerusalem is the exact opposite! There, the blood of countless substitutionary sacrifices flowed until the Son of God shed His blood on Calvary's cross.

Babylon says "No" to God but "Yes" to self, while Jerusalem, the City of Peace and the City of the Great King, says "Yes" to God and "No" to self.

Let's compare Babylon and Jerusalem:

Babylon vs. Jerusalem
Satan vs. God
Antichrist vs. Jesus Christ
The flesh vs. the Spirit

This helps us to better understand the battle and the time of Daniel. Daniel's time was very dangerous because the terrible, confusing amalgamation of Babylon and Jerusalem happened, *"And the Lord gave Jehoiakim king of Judah into his hand..."* (Daniel 1:2). Jerusalem ceased to be Jerusalem. The Lord gives only to the world what belongs to the world.

We're living in a similar perilous time today. This time in Earth's history is dangerous and highly explosive, not only because of nuclear, chemical and biological weapons, but also because of the spiritual amalgamation of Jerusalem and Babylon through the victory of the enemy in many churches and through the worldliness of millions of believers. If your heart has become Babylonish, if you're rejecting the cross, you may be a "Christian" outwardly, but in God's eyes, you're still united with Babylon, with the world.

The Consequence of Amalgamation

"And the Lord gave Jehoiakim king of Judah into his hand, with part of the vessels of the house of God: which he carried into the land of Shinar to the house of his god; and he brought the vessels into the treasure house of his god.

"And the king spake unto Ashpenaz the master of his eunuchs, that he should bring certain of the children of Israel, and of the king's seed, and of the princes;

"Children in whom was no blemish, but well favoured, and skilful in all wisdom, and cunning in knowledge, and

understanding science, and such as had ability in them to stand in the king's palace, and whom they might teach the learning and the tongue of the Chaldeans" (Daniel 1:2–4).

This is the terrible result of the amalgamation: Nebuchadnezzar took several vessels from the house of God and put them in the treasure house in the house of his god. The holy vessels were desecrated.

The Church of Jesus Christ, which is supposed to be a vessel for the glory of God, is desecrated in many places and it's permeated with the spirit of this world.

Hosea grieved, *"Israel is swallowed up: now shall they be among the Gentiles as a vessel wherein is no pleasure"* (Hosea 8:8).

We are warned in the Bible of this amalgamation and obliteration of borders which is taking place in our day, *"For this is the will of God...That every one of you should know how to possess his vessel in sanctification and honour"* (1st Thessalonians 4:3a and 4).

Are you a holy vessel?

Strangely, Daniel 1:2 says, *"...part of the vessels of the house of God..."* i.e., not all the vessels.

In the parable of the sower, it says of the seeds, *"Some fell by the wayside...some fell upon a rock...some fell among thorns...and other fell on good ground"* (Luke, chapter 8). Thirty-five percent of the seeds fell on good ground.

And we read in Revelation of the church at Sardis, *"Thou hast a few names even in Sardis which have not defiled their garments..."* (Revelation 3:4).

Thanks be to God for the "some," for the "few," for the "part of," for those who haven't let themselves be swept away by the spiritual currents of our time, and for those who are like the few believing young men of Israel who endured the Babylonian brainwashing but who didn't surrender to it.

It was drummed into them for three years that "only Babylon is good;" that "the Babylonian spirit is the only right one;" and that "Babylonian religion brings peace, enjoyment, and prosperity."

What type of men did Nebuchadnezzar, the king of Babylon, have his eyes on? Answer: *"Children of Israel...of the king's seed...in whom was no blemish."*

You too, child of God, are a target of the enemy. If you're born-again, you've become a king and a priest, without blemish, complete in Jesus Christ. The Bible says, *"There is therefore now no condemnation to them which are in Christ Jesus, who walk not after the flesh, but after the Spirit"* (Romans 8:1).

This is why the "king of Babylon" is so interested in you. He wants you to learn the "Chaldean teaching and language." That means he wants you to become assimilated and amalgamated with this world.

Hosts of Babylonian spirits are striving to indoctrinate Christians. The whole atmosphere is filled with Babylonian spirits of worldly lust today. Who'll go the way of the cross? Who'll flee out of Babylon? Only a few. It was also a very small remnant at the time of Nebuchadnezzar's reign which didn't want to be amalgamated. Of all the Jewish youths who had been brought up to learn the way of salvation so thoroughly, the majority allowed itself to be persuaded. Only four remained faithful. Do you belong to the few?

The Secret of Victory Over Amalgamation

"And the king appointed them a daily provision of the king's meat, and of the wine which he drank: so nourishing them three years, that at the end thereof they might stand before the king.

"Now among these were of the children of Judah, Daniel, Hananiah, Mishael, and Azariah" (Daniel 1:5–6).

The meaning of the names of the four youths are interesting. Daniel means "God is my judge"; Hananiah, "Jehovah is gracious"; Mishael, "Who is what God is?" ; and Azariah, "Jehovah helps."

These four young men are shining examples representing Israel in the midst of Babylon. They said "No" to amalgamation with the world. Their stand of faith cost them everything, but they endured. What was the secret of their victory? It's important for every Christian to know this.

The best promise for their victorious endurance had been established by their families. It says, *"Among these were of the children of Judah, Daniel, Hananiah, Mishael, and Azariah."* We as Christians also have a wonderful promise that will enable us to endure in this terrible time of the amalgamation of Jerusalem with Babylon.

If you're born-again, you also descend from "Judah," for it says in Hebrews 7:14, *"For it is evident that our Lord sprang out of Judah...."* You descend from Jesus. He is the first-born among many brethren. Blood bonds unite you with the Victor!

There's yet another promise, however, that equipped these young men to resist the temptation and remain faithful to the Lord: their holy resolution. *"But Daniel purposed in his heart that he would not defile himself with the portion of the king's meat, nor with the wine which he drank..."* (Daniel 1:8).

This drastic decision called for the young men to resist the will of King Nebuchadnezzar, and do the will of God. In verse 5 it says, *"And the king appointed them a daily provision of the king's meat...."* But, Daniel said "No" in his heart. Why was it so important to insist on saying "No"? Because he and his friends knew the will of God.

The Babylonians ate the meat with the blood sacrifices which were offered to idols, and the Israelites weren't allowed to do this. They could have no fellowship with Nebuchadnezzar.

"...What communion hath light with darkness?" asks Paul in 2nd Corinthians 6:14. Further, *"...the things which the Gentiles sacrifice, they sacrifice to devils, and not to God: and I would not that ye should have fellowship with devils"* (1st Corinthians 10:20).

For Daniel and his friends, a compromise was out of the question, for a compromise would have resulted in amalgamation with Babylon.

If you want to be a faithful child of God, then compromise—submitting to the spirit of this world—is impossible. If you do so, the result will be assimilation and amalgamation with Babylon. We have only two choices: the will of God or the will of Satan.

Why did God lead these young men into such a situation? There can only be one answer: So that He could prove Himself strongly to them and glorify Himself. *"For the eyes of the LORD run to and fro throughout the whole earth, to shew himself strong in the behalf of them whose heart is perfect toward him...."* (2nd Chronicles 16:9).

God saw Daniel and his friends. He saw the few men who were wholly on His side. Help comes after a total commitment to the Lord, not the other way round.

If you pray to the Lord half-heartedly in your battles, you can't expect help. Only if, like Daniel, at all costs you decide in your heart not to defile yourself, will the living God be with you.

Daniel 1:8 describes Daniel's decision, and in verse 9 we read, *"Now God had brought Daniel into favour and tender love with the prince of the eunuchs."* *"God had brought Daniel..."*! And in verse 17 we read, *"As for these four children, God gave them knowledge and skill in all learning and wisdom...."*

My dear reader, you, too, are living in a time of amalgamation. Nebuchadnezzar, the prince of this world, stands before you. He entices you with sensuality and immorality, prominence, opulence, and materialism, and he wants to lead you into compromise.

But behind you the Lord stands silent. The four youths were four among many, *"Among these were...Daniel, Hananiah, Mishael, and Azariah."* Many others who remain anonymous weren't mentioned again in the Bible because they compromised; they amalgamated with the spirit of Babylon. They had good food, good wine, and good lives, but they were useless to God.

The four faithful ones stood alone in their decision for the Lord, with the living God as their foundation. Those who compromised chose the way of least resistance, but they were erased from God's history book.

The four faithfully lived in great simplicity, but they had great honor. Later, they were even respected by the mighty Nebuchadnezzar. The others wanted to please the world, but they finished having no influence on it. The four faithful were foolish in the eyes of the others and in the eyes of the world, and yet Scripture says they were ten times wiser! They found true wisdom by offering their finished "Yes" to the Lord, the invisible God.

Unbelieving People
"And the king said unto them, I have dreamed a dream, and my spirit was troubled to know the dream" (Daniel 2:3). This short verse characterizes Nebuchadnezzar as an unbeliever. An unbeliever lives without God and is unstable. When something extraordinary happens, he's alarmed.

Nebuchadnezzar was at the height of his power as a mighty ruler, but where power is based on what's visible, there's no foundation. This became apparent when the invisible One intervened and wanted to speak to Nebuchad-nezzar. The ruler's whole existence was threatened, and he was extremely alarmed.

We see another example of this in the rich man described in Luke 12 who had lived all his life with only what he could see. He earned money and stored up material possessions, but he'd never seriously sought the invisible God. Then, he was shaken to the core because God said to him, *"Thou fool, this night thy soul shall be required of thee: then whose shall those things be, which thou hast provided?"* (Luke 12:20).

The unbeliever is also aimless in his actions. In Daniel 1, Nebuchadnezzar ordered that the Israelite youths were to be instructed in the Chaldean teaching and language for three years. Later, however, he commanded that they be executed with all the wise men of Babylon.

This is very relevant. The rich man in Luke 12 followed a zig-zag course because his life wasn't rooted in the living God. His actions were irrational and divided in opposite directions.

There are also "believing unbelievers" today who base their existence more on the earthly, the visible, than on the eternal, the invisible God. They believe in a theoretical Christ, but they're not rooted in Jesus. That's why they're so easily taken captive by the aimlessness and purposeless-ness of this world. They're vain in their words and actions. Jesus said of them, *"...these have no root..."* (Luke 8:13).

The unbelievers are also powerless to understand what God is saying. Nebuchadnezzar, the mighty king, was pow-erless because he didn't understand God. Deeply shocked by what his spirit had experienced, he awakened, *"...where-with his spirit was troubled, and his sleep brake from him"* (Daniel 2:1), but he couldn't interpret what had happened.

He sensed that the living God had spoken to him, but was unable to understand.

Only the impression that the revelation had made upon him remained, but it wasn't the revelation which he was to receive. How terrible!

God is also speaking today through His Word, showing Himself to the world. Everything is in motion today, everything is changing, but the "Nebuchadnezzars" of today don't understand. They make speeches, accuse others, travel around and hold conferences, but they don't have the answer. Has God also gotten your attention, through an accident or through sickness? Are you alarmed, but unable to understand what He wants to say to you through His Word?

The religious and wise men of Nebuchadnezzar's time were also unable to interpret the Lord's message because they, too, were unbelievers. They stood before Nebuchadnezzar and spoke, but they didn't have an explanation. They served idols; they had a religion, but not true faith in the God of the Bible.

Why do most Christians today have no answers to the world's questions? Why do we hear religious talk, but so little clear expository preaching of the Word of God? Answer: Because faith in Jesus is lacking. People believe in their churches, and in their Christian organizations, but they have no answers to the terrors of our time. They have no message and no vision.

It's frightening to see so little prophetic perspective today in preaching and testimony. But this is our message: Jesus is coming! If you're still clinging to the visible, if you as a believer are being ruled by money and possessions, then you have no message; you're merely talking. You have no vision.

You may say something theoretically, but you aren't speaking a living word with authority. That's what the world needs, however. Many who are in desperation and who want to take their own lives need the beloved Gospel.

The wise men in Babylon couldn't recognize the wisdom of God despite all their culture. They testified to their powerlessness, *"The Chaldeans answered before the king, and said, There is not a man upon the earth that can shew the king's matter: therefore there is no king, lord, nor ruler, that asked such things at any magician, or astrologer, or Chaldean.*

"And it is a rare thing that the king requireth, and there is none other that can shew it before the king, except the gods, whose dwelling is not with flesh" (Daniel 2:10–11).

The consequences for the religious and scientific leaders of that time were catastrophic: bitter rejection of their powerlessness by the world ruler, Nebuchadnezzar, who not only became very angry (verse 12), but also pronounced a death sentence upon them!

How we need revival today! The trashing of Christianity by a godless world happens because the world sees through the falsely-pious Christian facade. Paul says the people living in the last days will have *"...a form of godliness, but denying the power thereof"* (2nd Timothy 3:5).

Let me say this seriously: A judgment of death is hanging over religious Christians. In Revelation 2:5, the exalted Lord says, *"Remember therefore from whence thou art fallen, and repent, and do the first works; or else I will come unto thee quickly, and will remove thy candlestick out of his place, except thou repent."*

Powerlessness is the lack of authority, and the lack of authority is the result of hypocrisy in your life. Jesus said, *"...when the Son of man cometh, shall he find faith on the earth?"* (Luke 18:8).

In Babylon, God had men of faith in the midst of a world of unbelief. He had Daniel, who refused to compromise. It's a faith-filled, death-defying, confident statement that we read in Daniel 2:14–15a, *"Then Daniel answered with counsel and wisdom to Arioch the captain of the king's guard, which was gone forth to slay the wise men of Babylon:*

"He answered and said to Arioch the king's captain, Why is the decree so hasty from the king?..."

Here, Daniel took a step in faith. He was a God-fearing man, and he knew God would give him light in the midst of darkness. He defied death.

With it, he's a picture of our Lord Jesus Christ, who descended into this dark Babylon, conquered death, and brought life and immortality to us all.

What about you? You are to be like Jesus! You are to be a Daniel in the midst of Babylon. Defy, in the name of Jesus, the crashing waves of the powers of death, and claim the finished redemption! Begin to seek the face of God. Victory is assured through the Lord Jesus Christ!

Believing People

"Then Daniel went to his house, and made the thing known to Hananiah, Mishael, and Azariah, his companions:

"That they would desire mercies of the God of heaven concerning this secret; that Daniel and his fellows should not perish with the rest of the wise men of Babylon" (Daniel 2:17–18).

We've looked at Nebuchadnezzar, who personified unbelief. We'll now concern ourselves with Daniel, a man of faith in the midst of Babylon. What characteristics do his faith show to us? The characteristics of Jesus! Even Daniel knew of the substitutionary sacrifice. His faith was nourished by a living union with God through that sacrifice.

The first characteristic which we see in his faith is that of a priest. Daniel 2:13–14 says, *"And the decree went forth that the wise men should be slain; and they sought Daniel and his fellows to be slain.*

"Then Daniel answered..."

It's moving to see how Daniel stood as a substitute before the condemned wise men in Babylon. He says, *"Destroy not the wise men of Babylon: bring me in before the king, and I will shew unto the king the interpretation"* (Daniel 2:24).

Here, he's a picture of our Lord Jesus Christ. Daniel overcame, by faith, the one who had power over death: Nebuchadnezzar. He stopped him through the position he adopted. What does it say of Jesus in Hebrews 2:14? *"Forasmuch then as the children are partakers of flesh and blood, he also himself likewise took part of the same; that through death he might destroy him that had the power of death, that is, the devil."*

Just as Daniel stood before Nebuchadnezzar at the risk of his own life and annulled the death sentence, so Jesus confronted Satan and annulled death, *"O death, where is thy sting? O grave, where is thy victory?"* (1st Corinthians 15:55).

According to the Scriptures, we're also kings and priests (Revelation 1:6). Do you really stand in the gap as a priest? Do you snatch souls from the Devil through the power of the blood of Jesus Christ? Are you as a priest in prayer, like Daniel, who claimed the victory and prayed victoriously?

The second characteristic of Daniel's faith is that of a prophet. He was God's mouthpiece, *"Then was the secret revealed unto Daniel in a night vision. Then Daniel blessed the God of heaven"* (Daniel 2:19). He had a message for a desperate world. He knew God's plan.

What did his faith rest on? On the living God alone! Daniel had to learn this. In the beginning he had a "crutch." In Daniel chapter one, in which he ate "vegetables and drank water," he said to his friends, in effect, "The Lord can bless this." He reckoned with the food and drink besides the Lord. But now he had nothing left.

"...Daniel went to his house..." (Daniel 2:17). What did he have at home? A table and a chair—but he also had the living God. In God, there was vast power and authority. Daniel relied on the Lord alone. Nobody else could help.

All the others had failed. Nebuchadnezzar's power could not help; science was at a loss; the religious leaders had failed. Daniel only had the Lord, but that was enough.

The joy of the Lord is in having Him alone when all visible things collapse.

When the children of Israel stood by the Red Sea, God took all their supports away. Behind them were the Egyptians and before them the water. But God said, *"...Wherefore criest thou unto me? speak unto the children of Israel, that they go forward"* (Exodus 14:15).

"Where to, Lord?" Faith doesn't see the way. Faith sees the goal, the glory of the Lord. Think of Gideon, Abraham or David. They were all led to the point where they had no other help but God alone.

How was Daniel's faith strengthened? This is a great mystery. We see here in Babylon the first prayer meeting, *"Then Daniel went to his house, and made the thing known to Hananiah, Mishael, and Azariah, his companions:*

"That they would desire mercies of the God of heaven concerning this secret..." (Daniel 2:17–18a). How they must have wrestled in prayer that night, for that night the secret was revealed to Daniel in a vision.

Does your faith need strengthening? Do you need new boldness? Get down on your knees and pray aloud, based on Scripture, *"Ask, and it shall be given you; seek, and ye shall find; knock, and it shall be opened unto you"* (Matthew 7:7).

What was the expression of Daniel's faith? It was the victorious "He."

"Daniel answered and said, Blessed be the name of God for ever and ever: for wisdom and might are his: and HE

changeth the times and the seasons: HE removeth kings, and setteth up kings:

"HE giveth wisdom unto the wise, and knowledge to them that know understanding: HE revealeth the deep and secret things:

"HE knoweth what is in the darkness, and the light dwelleth with him" [emphasis ours] (Daniel 2:20–22).

It's as though Daniel forgot the pronoun "I." His praise and rejoicing didn't have himself as its object, but the Lord. Therefore, he could tangle with the power of unbelief and still be victorious, for it says in Daniel 2:46, *"Then the king Nebuchadnezzar fell upon his face, and worshipped Daniel...."* This is the victory of faith over Satan!

The Lord is looking for men and women today who, similar to Daniel, rely on Him alone, strengthen themselves in fellowship with like-minded brethren, deny themselves, and seek and praise Him!

Nebuchadnezzar's Dream

"Thou, O king, sawest, and behold a great image. This great image, whose brightness was excellent, stood before thee; and the form thereof was terrible.

"This image's head was of fine gold, his breast and his arms of silver, his belly and his thighs of brass, His legs of iron, his feet part of iron and part of clay.

"Thou sawest till that a stone was cut out without hands, which smote the image upon his feet that were of iron and clay, and brake them to pieces.

"Then was the iron, the clay, the brass, the silver, and the gold, broken to pieces together, and became like the chaff of the summer threshingfloors; and the wind carried them away, that no place was found for them: and the stone that smote the image became a great mountain, and filled the whole Earth.

"Forasmuch as thou sawest that the stone was cut out of the mountain without hands, and that it brake in pieces the iron, the brass, the clay, the silver, and the gold; the great God hath made known to the king what shall come to pass hereafter: and the dream is certain, and the interpretation thereof sure" (Daniel 2:31–35 and 45).

What exactly preceded the vision that God gave Nebuchadnezzar? Daniel 2:29 gives us the answer, *"As for thee, O king, thy thoughts came into thy mind upon thy bed, what should come to pass hereafter: and he that revealeth secrets maketh known to thee what shall come to pass."* These thoughts show us that despite his power, Nebuchadnezzar was very insecure and filled with foreboding and questions about the future, and often asking himself, "What will happen?"

It's just the same today. The Lord Jesus said of our time, *"...men's hearts [will fail] them for fear, and for looking after those things which are coming on the earth..."* (Luke 21:26).

Millions of people are asking, "What's going to happen?" Even the rulers of this Earth ask themselves secretly and fearfully, "What's going to happen?" despite their boasting and assurances that everything is under control. Nobody can give them a reliable answer. God alone gives the answer in His Word, but He wants instruments He can use to proclaim it. Daniel was such an instrument.

The characteristic of all true prophets of God is that they resist the temptation to become proud and to put themselves in the foreground.

Immediately after God starts to use a person, the demons of pride try to pounce on him. We see this in Daniel. When he stood before the king, the king asked him, *"...Art thou able to make known unto me the dream which I have seen, and the interpretation thereof?"* (Daniel 2:26).

Daniel resisted immediately, and answered, *"...The secret which the king hath demanded cannot the wise men, the astrologers, the magicians, the soothsayers, shew unto the king;*

"But there is a God in heaven that revealeth secrets..." (Daniel 2:27b–28a).

If you want to be a blessed instrument in the Lord's hand, then begin to resist, in the name of the Lord, your thirst for prestige. Then the Lord will be able to use you.

Let's consider the historical interpretation of Nebuchadnezzar's dream. *"Thou, O king, sawest, and behold a great image. This great image, whose brightness was excellent, stood before thee; and the form thereof was terrible"* (Daniel 2:31).

The prophesied world powers were terrifying. We know from historical sources that the kingdoms Daniel saw in the image were prophetically fulfilled in history. God speaks the truth in His Word! Daniel explained to Nebuchadnezzar, *"...Thou art this head of gold.*

"And after thee shall arise another kingdom inferior to thee..." (Daniel 2:38b-39a).

We know that the silver breast represented the Medo-Persian Empire; the belly of brass represented the Greek-Macedonian Empire of Alexander the Great; and the iron legs represented the hard Roman Empire. Were there other empires after the Roman Empire? Yes, but God shows us world history as seen from Israel.

Only those empires which ruled over Israel are enumerated because of their spiritual meaning.

Let's consider the importance of the last empire, the Roman Empire, as described in Daniel 2:40–43 in great detail. Why is this? Because the first phase of the Roman Empire, the legs of iron, is connected with the First Coming of Jesus. The Son of God came to Earth during the time of the Roman Empire. Jesus Christ was condemned by a Roman governor and nailed to a Roman cross by Romans.

But, He reconciled the world with God, rose again and ascended into heaven during the time of the Roman Empire, and He'll return to Israel when the last phase of the restoration of the Roman Empire begins.

This is why the last phase of the Roman Empire is so interesting. It's described in Daniel 2:41, *"And whereas thou sawest the feet and toes, part of potters' clay, and part of iron, the kingdom shall be divided; but there shall be in it of the strength of the iron, forasmuch as thou sawest the iron mixed with miry clay."* Iron and clay can't be mixed. They have no common properties and can't be combined successfully.

Today, the time of the Gentile nations is ending. The Bible teaches clearly that there will be no lasting peace until the Prince of Peace, Jesus Christ, comes.

If we look closely at the image that Nebuchadnezzar saw in his dream, we see the increasing devaluation of the empires: gold, silver, brass, iron, iron and clay. This process of degeneration is progressing to the time when the stone cut out of the mountain without hands will smash the image of the nations and fill the whole world (Daniel 2:44–45). That's the return of Jesus Christ at Armageddon when He'll crush the enemies of Israel.

According to our understanding of the Scriptures, the ten toes on the feet of the image, which are partly of iron and partly of clay, represent the Roman Empire, united Europe, which is taking on even clearer contours. The rise of Rome in the religious, political and economic sphere is a fact today.

During the Second World War, British Prime Minister Winston Churchill, who was well known for his vision of the future, warned of a united Europe and the associated

dangers. I can't go any further into this, but I'd remind you
of 2nd Peter 1:19 where it's written, *"We have also a more
sure word of prophecy; whereunto ye do well that ye take
heed, as unto a light that shineth in a dark place, until the
day dawn, and the day star arise in your hearts."*

Planet Earth is becoming very dark spiritually. Only
those who have the light of the prophetic Word can recognize clearly the shape of its fulfillment.

I believe that the iron and clay also point to the relationship of Israel to the nations. Just as iron and clay can't be
mixed, Israel was never lost in the nations; she was never
assimilated and won't be fully assimilated in the coming
anti-Christian era.

In Jeremiah 18:1–6, Israel is called "clay." According to
Isaiah 28:15–16, she will make a pact with hell, a pact with
the Antichrist, the ruler of the nations, but this pact will be
broken in the Great Tribulation.

Iron and clay also represent the Christianity of the endtimes which seeks to amalgamate with the world in various
places. Thus, the church has become conformed to the
world. But, the Lord says "No" to this mixture (1st John
2:15–17).

Then the "stone," Jesus, will come. It's later than most
people think. Daniel said to Nebuchadnezzar, *"And in the
days of these kings shall the God of heaven set up a kingdom, which shall never be destroyed: and the kingdom shall
not be left to other people, but it shall break in pieces and
consume all these kingdoms, and it shall stand for ever"*
(Daniel 2:44).

The image of the nations is already beginning to topple;
the Babylonian confusion of languages is devastating. If we
hold the Bible to our ear, we hear already the stone cut out
of the mountain without hands coming nearer. Jesus is coming! Prepare to meet Him!

The Scriptures say, *"Follow peace with all men, and holiness, without which no man shall see the Lord"* (Hebrews 12:14).

Nebuchadnezzar's Dream—
Its Significance For Christians

"And whereas thou sawest iron mixed with miry clay, they shall mingle themselves with the seed of men: but they shall not cleave one to another, even as iron is not mixed with clay" (Daniel 2:43).

We've already seen the ten toes of iron and clay as a united Europe and its relationship to Israel. The precept that clay and iron can't be mixed also applies to you, for that which is happening in the nations is also taking place in the hearts of separate people. Just as in the universe, in its infinity, millions of planets continually revolve in their tracks, we find the same principle in the smallest invisible atom.

What does Isaiah 64:8 say? *"But now, O LORD, thou art our father; we are the clay, and thou our potter; and we all are the work of thy hand."*

This truth has spoken to me in a new way. As a child of God, you don't belong with the iron of this world. Don't you see that this amalgamation in your life isn't profitable? You're in great danger in these endtimes if you compromise with the spirit of this world, if you're materialistically minded and seek honor and prominence. The Scriptures say, *"For our conversation is in heaven; from whence also we look for the Saviour, the Lord Jesus Christ"* (Philippians 3:20).

You're the clay; you belong in the Potter's hands. His nail-pierced hands want to make a vessel out of your life, a holy vessel for His honor.

Maybe you're saying, "His efforts with me are in vain. I'm a marred vessel." Then turn to Jeremiah 18:3–4, *"Then*

*I went down to the potter's house, and, behold, he wrought
a work on the wheels.*

*"And the vessel that he made of clay was marred in the
hand of the potter: so he made it again another vessel, as
seemed good to the potter to make it."*

There was a crack or a hard spot in the clay. Did the potter throw the marred vessel away? No. It says, *"...so he
made it again another vessel, as seemed good to the potter
to make it."* He made a beautiful vessel out of the marred
one. Who did this? The hands of the Master!

Jesus said that you are in His hand, and no one will ever
pluck you out of His hand (see John 10:28).

How can you become a vessel that's pleasing to Him?
You only have to be still in the Master's hand. You must let
Him form you, knead you and turn you. Say "Yes" to His
ways, to the fire of suffering. He doesn't want you, His clay,
to become mixed with the iron of this world which is ripe
for judgment, for He doesn't want you to be destroyed with
it at His coming as the stone cut out of the mountain without hands.

This is why Jeremiah 51:6 says, *"Flee out of the midst of
Babylon, and deliver every man his soul: be not cut off in
her iniquity; for this is the time of the LORD'S vengeance;
he will render unto her a recompence."*

Worship with the Prophet Isaiah, *"But now, O LORD,
thou art our father; we are the clay, and thou our potter;
and we all are the work of thy hand"* (Isaiah 64:8).

This attitude is of vital importance if you're a child of
God, for the "stone" will destroy the nations at
Armageddon. Are you still clinging to the iron of the world,
or are you in His nail-pierced hands?

What simple pictures the Holy Spirit uses to proclaim the
greatest truths to us! Jesus—the stone. What's more trivial
than a stone? Look at the shining golden head of the image

of nations: How imposing it looks to the human eye, and yet it's nothing (Isaiah 40:15).

The Apostle Paul wrote, *"While we look not at the things which are seen, but at the things which are not seen: for the things which are seen are temporal; but the things which are not seen are eternal"* (2nd Corinthians 4:18).

According to 1st Peter 2:4, Jesus is a living stone. He'll remain in eternity. Nebuchadnezzar and all the "Nebuchadnezzars" since have disappeared, but Jesus remains. Are you united with Him? Don't forget that He's the stone that was rejected by the builders (1st Peter 2:4 and 7). The religious builders of today also often reject the stone, Jesus Christ, for it says in 1st Peter 2:8 that He's *"...a stone of stumbling, and a rock of offence, even to them which stumble at the word...."*

This is the preaching of the cross, which is foolishness to those that perish, but the power of God to us who are saved (1st Corinthians 1:18). This stone which is cut out without hands will soon fill the whole world.

It's a stone of decision, Daniel says, *"And in the days of these kings shall the God of heaven set up a kingdom, which shall never be destroyed: and the kingdom shall not be left to other people, but it shall break in pieces and consume all these kingdoms, and it shall stand for ever.*

"Forasmuch as thou sawest that the stone was cut out of the mountain without hands, and that it brake in pieces the iron, the brass, the clay, the silver, and the gold..." (Daniel 2:44–45a).

This stone is also a stone of decision for you, however. If you turn in your Bible to Luke 20, you'll find the confirmation of this in verses 17 and 18, *"And he beheld them, and said, What is this then that is written, The stone which the builders rejected, the same is become the head of the corner?*

"Whosoever shall fall upon that stone shall be broken; but on whomsoever it shall fall, it will grind him to powder."

Jesus is looking at you now. He's the stone of stumbling and a rock of offence to you deep down in your heart, if you don't want to exchange your old nature for the cross. Do you, as clay, still want to amalgamate with the iron of the world? *"For yet a little while, and he that shall come will come, and will not tarry"* (Hebrews 10:37). Surrender yourself anew as clay to His nail-pierced hands. Break yourself from the iron of the world.

Nebuchadnezzar As A Type

"Then an herald cried aloud, To you it is commanded, O people, nations, and languages,

"That at what time ye hear the sound of the cornet, flute, harp, sackbut, psaltery, dulcimer, and all kinds of musick, ye fall down and worship the golden image that Nebuchadnezzar the king hath set up:

"And whoso falleth not down and worshippeth shall the same hour be cast into the midst of a burning fiery furnace" (Daniel 3:4–6).

Summarized in one sentence, Nebuchadnezzar is a picture of the incarnate Satan, the Beast, the Antichrist. Daniel 3:4–6, therefore, has the same meaning as Revelation 13:14–15. What was Nebuchadnezzar? He was a world ruler. The Bible calls Satan the "prince of this world."

Although the Lord is the King of heaven and Earth, and all judgment is given over to Jesus, Satan was judged on Calvary's cross, but the Lord hasn't executed him yet. God lets Satan be the prince of this world so that man can decide, just as Adam and Eve did in the Garden.

The three youths in Daniel 3 knew that the prince of darkness who was visible to them, Nebuchadnezzar, had made a claim on their lives.

But the invisible Prince of light is silent and waits to see who'll turn to Him, the Lord, or to the Nebuchadnezzars of this world. Today, we are in the same situation. We're living in an anti-Christian time. It's a time for you to decide. Everyone is taking part in this battle, including Christians. We can't simply sit down and rest and wait for heaven; we're living in a time similar to Nebuchadnezzar's.

The spirit of the Antichrist is spreading today, and we must take up a very decided position.

What was Nebuchadnezzar's aim? Just as Satan wants us to acknowledge him as God and ruler, Nebuchadnezzar commanded that *"...ye fall down and worship the golden image...."*

The Devil's aim from the beginning has always been to be like God and to overthrow Him. Throughout the centuries, Satan has been striving to gain dominion over men and women. He even wanted the dominion over Jesus, the Son of God, in the wilderness, *"Again, the devil taketh him up into an exceeding high mountain, and sheweth him all the kingdoms of the world, and the glory of them;*

"And saith unto him, All these things will I give thee, if thou wilt fall down and worship me.

"Then saith Jesus unto him, Get thee hence, Satan: for it is written, Thou shalt worship the Lord thy God, and him only shalt thou serve" (Matthew 4:8–10).

Let's see this clearly. Satan wants to get every single person under his rule, as it says in 2nd Timothy 2:26. Satan's will is very relentless. We'll only survive and be able to resist his will if we're equally decided in our turning to God.

What was the purpose of the worship of the image which Nebuchadnezzar commanded?

First, it was the denial of God's total claim to us, the setting aside of the rule of God. The worship of an image is affirming what's visible—the lust of the eyes.

Whoever is guided by the visible and temporal—by money, possessions, honor—will come under judgment, for *"...the world passeth away, and the lust thereof: but he that doeth the will of God abideth for ever"* (1st John 2:17).

The worship of the image—gold—is also the lust of the flesh:

"For all that is in the world, the lust of the flesh (gold), *and the lust of the eyes* (the image, the visible), *and the pride of life* (rejection of the rulership of God), *is not of the Father, but is of the world"* (1st John 2:16).

Who worshipped the image? Those who did the will of Satan instead of the will of God. Those who do the will of Satan can be identified by the following characteristics:

—Pride: Those who are touchy should know that they're proud, for the Devil is also proud.

— The pride of life: A wish for worldly pleasures, enjoyments and passions.

— The lust of the eyes: Those who are compelled to do things they don't want to do are actually worshipping Satan.

Are you compelled to smoke, drink, curse or lie? Are you compelled to be immoral? Then you've bowed your knees to the golden image. You're standing outside the holy, saving will of God and are captive to the will of Satan.

If Nebuchadnezzar is, on the one hand, man, and on the other hand, a type of Satan, who does he actually portray?

The man of sin, the Antichrist, whose spirit is beginning to permeate the world today, who's already brought millions of people under his power through occultism, spiritism and clairvoyance!

Revelation 13:18 says, *"Here is wisdom. Let him that hath understanding count the number of the beast: for it is the number of a man; and his number is Six hundred threescore and six."* Six is the utmost which man can achieve. Man is the creation of the sixth day. Goliath, the mocker of God, was six cubits tall; his spearhead had a weight of six hundred shekels of iron and he was armed with six weapons (1st Samuel 17).

And Nebuchadnezzar's image? *"Nebuchadnezzar the king made an image of gold, whose height was threescore cubits, and the breadth thereof six cubits"* (Daniel 3:1). Verses 5, 10 and 15 mention six instruments which were played in the worship of the image. Let's go deeper into this matter. How did Nebuchadnezzar become an Antichrist?

Here the original sin is shown: Nebuchadnezzar used the divine light that the Lord gave him for his own glorification. God had given him a dream of revelation. Daniel said, *"...Thou art this head of gold"* (Daniel 2:38).

Instead of humbling himself then and surrendering to God, Nebuchadnezzar acted like Satan.

He became a picture of Satan, who had also been clothed by God with great glory and majesty, but who then exalted himself, *"...I will exalt my throne above the stars of God"* (Isaiah 14:13b). This is Antichrist. Nebuchadnezzar used religion for his own glory and idolatry.

Religion with the aim of self-glorification is anti-Christian. The man who says, "I'm a good man" is like the first antichrist, Cain, who was religious, built an altar and sacrificed on it, but didn't bring a substitute as Abel did, with it humbling himself before God and confessing his sins. Cain, instead, brought his *own* gift.

Christianity today is often mere outward form and does not accept the living Christ. It becomes anti-Christianity. We're living in a very serious time.

John wrote in his letter, *"Little children, it is the last time: and as ye have heard that Antichrist shall come, even now are there many antichrists; whereby we know that it is the last time"* (1st John 2:18).

Where Satan can push Jesus out of the center in a Christian's life, that person himself becomes the center. Examine yourself in the light of God. Is your ego in the center of your life? Then you have a connection to the Antichrist. I want to ask you in Christ's stead to bow your knees and say to the Lord, "Not I, but Christ" and "All for Jesus," for only in this way and with this attitude can we overcome in this anti-Christian time.

A Sixfold Temptation

"Shadrach, Meshach, and Abednego, answered and said to the king, O Nebuchadnezzar, we are not careful to answer thee in this matter.

"If it be so, our God whom we serve is able to deliver us from the burning fiery furnace, and he will deliver us out of thine hand, O king.

"But if not, be it known unto thee, O king, that we will not serve thy gods, nor worship the golden image which thou hast set up" (Daniel 3:16–18).

We see from the example of the three youths, Daniel's friends, how we can victoriously resist the spreading anti-Christianity: through full surrender to the living God.

The Apostle Paul said, *"I beseech you therefore, brethren, by the mercies of God, that ye present your bodies a living sacrifice, holy, acceptable unto God, which is your reasonable service"* (Romans 12:1).

This full surrender to the living God gave the young men the strength to defy the threat. They were in danger. They stood before the alternative: either the golden image or the fiery furnace.

Today, the choice is Christ or Antichrist. Satan doesn't spare believers—on the contrary!

Because the three young men were totally devoted to the Lord, they could say "No" to the subtle attempts of the "Antichrist" to draw them over to his side. *"Put on the whole armour of God, that ye may be able to stand against the wiles of the devil"* (Ephesians 6:11). This is the Apostle Paul's advice to us!

Nebuchadnezzar made six attempts to make Daniel's three friends worship the image:

First, he tempted them with the gold which shined so radiantly and which had a mysterious attraction for the Babylonians. The image in the plain of Dura must have been very imposing.

In a similar fashion today, "gold" also causes Christians to act anti-Christian. It makes them materialistic and money worshippers instead of true worshippers of God in spirit and in truth. The fact that you may have money is irrelevant, but if the money has you, it's fatal!

Nebuchadnezzar's second effort to make the three youths worship the statue involved the influence of the masses, for all the princes and governors, really all Nebuchadnezzar's subjects, had to bow down before the image.

The enemy also tries this with you. He says, in effect, "If all the others are doing it, you can do it too. Your parents do it, your family. Who are you to be different? We're all brothers who seek a 'dialogue' with one another. It can only be good, such wonderful unity. We have to be tolerant for the sake of love."

Satan's influence on the masses is perilous today. We can only stand firm if we surrender ourselves to the living God. Only in this way can we discern the evil and remain on God's pathway.

Nebuchadnezzar's third effort to influence the youths was through music. *"That at what time ye hear the sound of the cornet, flute, harp, sackbut, psaltery, dulcimer, and all kinds of musick, ye fall down and worship the golden image that Nebuchadnezzar the king hath set up"* (Daniel 3:5). When we hear worldly music, particularly rock music, we understand how it stimulates the undiscerning and acts like a drug on lost souls. The three young men withstood this temptation.

A fourth way the king gave the youths reason to surrender was through the mockery and envy of anti-Semitism. *"Wherefore at that time certain Chaldeans came near, and accused the Jews"* (Daniel 3:8).

Enmity, envy and jealousy of the Chaldeans had been present for a long while because the young men who walked in faith were highly respected by the king. But the youths didn't allow themselves to be intimidated by this resistance, and they didn't worship the image.

Why do you let yourself, then, be intimidated so quickly by mockery or resistance from your colleagues and acquaintances? Take your stand for Jesus and you'll be a victor in this, too!

Fifth, the king unleashed his wrath in a plan to force the young men to worship the image, *"Then was Nebuchadnezzar full of fury, and the form of his visage was changed against Shadrach, Meshach, and Abednego..."* (Daniel 3:19). Yet, they weren't afraid. They had dedicated themselves to the Lord and those who do this aren't afraid (Psalm 3:27). They victoriously withstood the wrath of the king.

Sixth, the king tried to flatter the youths to induce them to compromise. At their first resistance, he spoke with them in a friendly manner and said, *"Now if ye be ready that at what time ye hear the sound of the cornet, flute, harp, sack-*

but, psaltery, and dulcimer, and all kinds of musick, ye fall down and worship the image which I have made; well..." (Daniel 3:15).

But not even this flattery would work. They withstood all enticements and threats. Why? Because they were dedicated to God! There lies the secret of victoriously resisting the temptation to compromise.

If a Christian isn't fully dedicated to the Lord, the anti-Christian spirit will take hold of him. Hasten, therefore, to surrender yourself to the Lord fully.

Let's ask ourselves the question, "How can we glorify Jesus Christ in the midst of anti-Christianity?" To resist is negative, but to glorify Jesus Christ is a divine opportunity.

Let's consider these three young men. How did they glorify the Lord? Through finished trust in the eternal God! Only through such trust can we have a credible testimony before the visible and invisible world.

Daniel's three young friends weren't timid and feeble in their answer, but they said with firm conviction, *"...be it known unto thee, O king, that we will not serve thy gods, nor worship the golden image which thou hast set up"* (Daniel 3:18). This statement was unmistakably clear.

The three were capable through their whole dedication of their lives to the honor of their Lord. They must have known the promise of God in Isaiah 43:2, *"When thou passest through the waters, I will be with thee; and through the rivers, they shall not overflow thee: when thou walkest through the fire, thou shalt not be burned; neither shall the flame kindle upon thee."*

Is it clear to you now that the Lord lets you be cast into the fiery furnace of suffering so that His name can be glorified through you?

Are you fully dedicated to the Lord? Are you trusting Him wholly? If you can say "Yes" with all your heart, then don't fear the furnace of testing and suffering, because then you'll become like Jesus!

The Seven-Fold Significance of the Fiery Furnace

"Therefore because the king's commandment was urgent, and the furnace exceeding hot, the flame of the fire slew those men that took up Shadrach, Meshach, and Abednego.

"And these three men, Shadrach, Meshach, and Abednego, fell down bound into the midst of the burning fiery furnace" (Daniel 3:22–23).

What does the fiery furnace represent, prophetically speaking? First, it's the center of this whole event, for those who wouldn't worship Nebuchadnezzar's golden image stood in the center of the glowing, threatening furnace of judgment—like the cross of Calvary.

Whoever won't worship the Antichrist, whoever won't do the will of Satan, will have one alternative: "the fiery furnace." This furnace, however, was the young men's salvation, despite how contradictory this may seem.

Second, you may also realize now that the place of judgment, where Jesus Christ died on the cross for your sins, is a place of salvation.

This is the central point of our message, for we're determined *"...not to know any thing among you, save Jesus Christ, and him crucified"* (1st Corinthians 2:2).

The fiery furnace was, furthermore, the place where the whole fury of Nebuchadnezzar came upon these faithful witnesses of the living God.

When Jesus hung on the cross, the fury of hell came upon Him because He carried away the sins of the world. When He cried in His agony, *"My God, my God, why hast thou forsaken me?"* hell pounced on Him in immeasurable rage.

It says in Daniel 3:19, *"Then was Nebuchadnezzar full of fury, and the form of his visage was changed against*

Shadrach, Meshach, and Abednego: therefore he spake, and commanded that they should heat the furnace one seven times more than it was wont to be heated."

Here, we have the third meaning of the fiery furnace. How many times hotter did the king's servants have to heat the furnace? Seven times!

The number "seven" shows divine completion. On the seventh day God "rested from" His work of creation. When we find the number seven in our Bible, we see the finished work of God. This is why the fiery furnace is also the place where God did His work, as on the cross, *"...God was in Christ, reconciling the world unto himself..."* (2nd Corinthians 5:19).

If you accept the cross for yourself, if you're willing to go into the fiery furnace with your old life, you'll experience the complete work of God. Then He'll say of your life, *"...Behold, I make all things new..."* (Revelation 21:5).

Fourth, the fiery furnace is the place where our worst and most dangerous enemies are removed and defeated, *"Therefore because the king's commandment was urgent, and the furnace exceeding hot, the flame of the fire slew those men that took up Shadrach, Meshach, and Abednego"* (Daniel 3:22). According to verse 20, these men were the mightiest in Nebuchadnezzar's army, and they wanted to destroy Shadrach, Meshach and Abednego. But, *they* perished in the flames!

As a born-again Christian, why do you fear? Don't you know that in Jesus Christ you're unconquerable? As long as you remain in the "fiery furnace" with Him, the strongest enemies can't touch you! Paul rejoiced over this, *"But thanks be to God, which giveth us the victory through our Lord Jesus Christ"* (1st Corinthians 15:57).

The secret of continual victory is to remain in the death of Jesus, in the fiery furnace: *"I am crucified with*

Christ..." (Galatians 2:20). You have no final reason, therefore, to be despondent. Salvation, the victory of Jesus, is
unlimited for those who'll remain in Him.

How wonderful to see these three youths being untouchable by the enemy because they consciously took the path of
faith. You'll also remain untouchable by the enemy as long
as you resist him in faith and willingly take the path of the
"fiery furnace."

Fifth, this fiery furnace was a place from which the Devil
had to flee, because it became a place of salvation. *"Then
Nebuchadnezzar the king was aston[ished], and rose up in
haste..."* (Daniel 3:24a). This cruel ruler became weak and
miserable, filled with fear and trembling, when he saw the
furnace.

He even began to praise the God of heaven. Satan trem-
bles when he sees the weakest saint upon his knees. These
youths experienced the truth of the words of James
4:7b–8a, *"...Resist the devil, and he will flee from you.
Draw nigh to God, and he will draw nigh to you...."*

Sixth, the furnace is the only place where Jesus walks
with us visibly. Nebuchadnezzar said in Daniel 3:24b–25,
*"...Did not we cast three men bound into the midst of the
fire? They answered and said unto the king, True, O king.*

*"He answered and said, Lo, I see four men loose, walk-
ing in the midst of the fire, and they have no hurt; and the
form of the fourth is like the Son of God."*

The Son of God walked with them in the fiery furnace.
Jesus is never as close to us as on the cross. There the Lamb
is shown. In the surrender of your old life, Jesus shows
Himself to you. All knowledge of Jesus Christ apart from
the cross of Calvary is purely theoretical knowledge and
leads to death. Those who subject their lives to the fiery furnace, however, experience Jesus walking with them even
there!

Finally, seventh, this fiery furnace is the place where, by surrendering our own lives, we receive them anew, as it says in Romans 6:5, *"For if we have been planted together in the likeness of his death, we shall be also in the likeness of his resurrection."*

The young men came unharmed, new and unconquerable, out of the fiery furnace, and even Nebuchadnezzar began to worship the Lord. What will you choose? The golden image or the fiery furnace? Christ or the Antichrist?

Belshazzar's Feast

"Belshazzar the king made a great feast to a thousand of his lords, and drank wine before the thousand."

"They drank wine, and praised the gods of gold, and of silver, of brass, of iron, of wood, and of stone.

"In the same hour came forth fingers of a man's hand, and wrote over against the candlestick upon the plaister of the wall of the king's palace: and the king saw the part of the hand that wrote" (Daniel 5:1 and 4–5).

In this chapter, we have another prophetic event before us. It's shocking to see in it how hardened a person's heart can be. Let's consider first the political-prophetic aspect of the event. In the night of Belshazzar's feast, the Babylonian empire fell and the Persians seized power.

The Babylonian ruler was totally unaware of the impending doom. Also, today, the nations are fully unaware of the approaching judgment and seizing of power from above. So, we want to proclaim loudly: The people of Israel are the writing on the wall for the nations! *"...Thou art weighed in the balances, and art found wanting"* (verse 27).

God is turning from the Gentiles and is beginning to bless Israel. What we see in this passage at the end of the *first* world empire, we're also seeing now at the end of the *last* world empire.

This is why the Bible says, *"Flee out of the midst of Babylon, and deliver every man his soul: be not cut off in her iniquity..."* (Jeremiah 51:6a). Have you fled out of Babylon? Have you broken with the spirit of this world? Jesus is coming soon, but He'll be followed by terrible judgments in the Tribulation period!

Holy and Unholy
We also see, however, the religious-prophetic aspect of this event. King Belshazzar, with his thousand lords, committed a great, thoughtless sin at his feast, namely the mixing of the holy with the unholy.

In Daniel 5:2–3, we read that he had the golden and silver vessels brought which his father, Nebuchadnezzar, had stolen from the Temple in Jerusalem and desecrated with his princes, wives and concubines. What a perverse and blasphemous thing to do!

This is also happening today, even among Christians. Have you mixed the holy with the unholy? The Lord laments in Ezekiel 22:26, *"...they have put no difference between the holy and profane, neither have they shewed difference between the unclean and the clean...."* This is the abominable sin of obliterated borders.

If you're born-again, you're a holy vessel in God's eyes. If this vessel is filled with impure thoughts and imaginations, however, you're committing the same sin as Belshazzar.

For example, if the love of God has been poured out in your heart and you still hate your brother, you are in darkness, just as you are if you criticize your pastor unscripturally, however holy your words may sound.

Or, if you pray and yet continue to lust in your heart after sinful things, then you're not differentiating between the holy and the unholy.

There's only one thing for you to do: repent! We're living at a serious time, for Jesus is coming soon! The world and the nations are unaware of this. They don't see the writing on the wall!

Let's look also at the personal aspect of this prophetic event concerning Belshazzar, the son of Nebuchadnezzar. There are four things about him worth mentioning.

First, he was a typical endtime person. Jesus mentions them in Matthew 24:38 in His description of Noah's time, *"For as in the days that were before the flood they were eating and drinking, marrying and giving in marriage...."* It was as though Belshazzar wanted to fill his inner emptiness with pleasure, feasting and sin.

Are you such a person, one who always has to be distracted by something so that you can forget your emptiness? Do you run from one thing to another, desperately unhappy despite your religion?

Second, Belshazzar knew the divine truth, seeing the conversion of his father. God humbled Nebuchadnezzar, and he testified afterwards,

"Now I Nebuchadnezzar praise and extol and honour the King of heaven, all whose works are truth, and his ways judgment: and those that walk in pride he is able to abase" (Daniel 4:37).

Although Belshazzar knew this from childhood, he was not obedient. The Bible says, *"...they all might be damned who believed not the truth, but had pleasure in unrighteousness"* (2nd Thessalonians 2:12). Here, we surely have the reason Belshazzar didn't apply the truth to his own life: his lust for sin was great. What were his sins?

One sin was the original sin which is in all of us: rebellion against the living God, the hidden, Satanic contamination of what's holy. Immorality also was a sin of Belshazzar. We see in many things how decadent people were then.

Then, he committed the sin of gluttony. These are the amusements of the endtimes: eating, drinking, marrying, divorcing and remarrying. It's our "I will" against God's holy "I will."

Third, Belshazzar was unaware that he was besieged. While the enemy began to slip in, he was celebrating. It's often alarming to see how people, even believers, are unaware of what's happening. Don't you see that today we're experiencing an invasion of spirits from below? We need repentance, prayer, and a cry to God to grant us more grace!

Fourth, Belshazzar crossed the border of God's longsuffering. Daniel said to him later, *"And thou his son, O Belshazzar, hast not humbled thine heart, though thou knewest all this"* (Daniel 5:22).

Although he knew the truth, he worshipped idols with holy vessels in his hands (Daniel 5:4).

Then, it says in verse 5, *"In the same hour came forth fingers of a man's hand, and wrote over against the candlestick upon the plaister of the wall of the king's palace...."*

Those who stubbornly cling to "idols of gold, silver, wood or stone" after they've recognized the truth, and who don't surrender themselves to the Lord, are beginning to cross the border.

Daniel 5:7–9 shows us that neither the soothsayers, astrologers, or Chaldeans could interpret the writing. They did not understand.

The question now is, "Do we understand?" Do you see the writing on the wall—Israel? Jesus is coming! The world is collapsing now because of the spiritual rot, supported only by lies and fabrications.

The spiritual writing on the wall is recorded in Revelation 2:4–5, *"Nevertheless I have somewhat against thee, because thou hast left thy first love.*

"Remember therefore from whence thou art fallen, and repent, and do the first works; or else I will come unto thee quickly, and will remove thy candlestick out of his place, except thou repent."

Of Belshazzar it says, *"Thou...hast not humbled thine heart."* Only humbling ourselves can help us, for the Scriptures tell us, *"Humble yourselves therefore under the mighty hand of God..."* (1st Peter 5:6).

In humbling yourself before Him, at the cross, you'll experience, as it's also written in the Bible, that the writing that was against you is blotted out (Colossians 2:14). Let the blood of the Lamb, Jesus Christ, cleanse you from all sin!

Weighted In the Balances and Found Wanting

"And this is the writing that was written, MENE, MENE, TEKEL, UPHARSIN.

"This is the interpretation of the thing: MENE; God hath numbered thy kingdom, and finished it.

"TEKEL; Thou art weighed in the balances, and art found wanting.

"PERES; Thy kingdom is divided, and given to the Medes and Persians" (Daniel 5:25–28).

The great tragedy in the life of Belshazzar is that he was almost saved. All the signs of true, saving repentance were present. When he saw the writing appearing on the wall, it says, *"Then the king's countenance was changed, and his thoughts troubled him, so that the joints of his loins were loosed, and his knees smote one against another"* (Daniel 5:6).

He even lost his composure, *"The king cried aloud..."* (verse 7). When he found that not one of his wise men could interpret the writing, it says, *"Then was king Belshazzar greatly troubled, and his countenance was changed in him..."* (verse 9).

This is a sign of conversion, because he was gripped by the fear of God, and the Scriptures say that the fear of the Lord tendeth to life, indeed, is a source of life. It is the beginning of conversion. Belshazzar got that far.

In Daniel 5:17–28 we read how Daniel confronted the king's son with his sins and interpreted the writing on the wall, *"...Thou art weighed in the balances, and art found wanting."*

Belshazzar's condition was hopeless! The enemy had surrounded the city, and yet he would have been saved if he had only done the one right thing: if he had humbled himself. The salvation of the sinner lies in the one Scripture, *"...Humble yourselves therefore under the mighty hand of God."*

When the idolatrous King Manasseh waited in fear in prison and began to cry to God, weeping and humbling himself, the Lord had mercy upon him.

When the persecutor of the church, Saul of Tarsus, broke down and humbled himself, the Lord made him His servant.

When King David became an adulterer and a murderer, but fell down before God and humbled himself, the Lord restored him.

When the Apostle Peter denied his Saviour and Jesus looked at him, he humbled himself and wept bitterly, then he also found grace again.

I can also personally testify that my Christian life came to a turning point when I humbled myself by the grace of God under His mighty hand. Everything became new and different after that.

Are you one of the many religious "Belshazzars" in that you have sinned and mixed the holy with the unholy? Have you been impure? Do not continue, then, in your wrongdoing, but humble yourself under the mighty hand of God, and He will exalt you.

The Tragedy

Who prevented Belshazzar from humbling himself? In the first place, his own mother. Daniel 5:10 says, *"Now the queen by reason of the words of the king and his lords came into the banquet house: and the queen spake and said, O king, live for ever: let not thy thoughts trouble thee, nor let thy countenance be changed."* Belshazzar's fear and willingness to repent diminished as result. Perhaps your relatives stand between you and real repentance. Perhaps your "Christian" brothers and sisters abuse the grace of God by saying, "God is a God of love," thereby winking at sin, ignoring the fact that God is also holy and just. Belshazzar was too embarrassed to repent in front of his thousand lords. His pride prevented him.

What about you? Do you see the writing on the wall over your life? If you were tried now, would you be *"...weighed in the balances, and ...found wanting"*?

After Belshazzar heard Daniel's call to repent, he wanted to retain his royal dignity, and did not want to break with sin. Daniel 5:29 says, *"Then commanded Belshazzar, and they clothed Daniel with scarlet, and put a chain of gold about his neck, and made a proclamation concerning him, that he should be the third ruler in the kingdom."*

How terrible, for the next verse says, *"In that night was Belshazzar the king of the Chaldeans slain."* He had not repented. Therefore, do not ignore the call to humble yourself before God. In humbling yourself you will experience the cleansing of the blood of Jesus. Accept the judgment of the cross upon your sinful life. In humbling yourself you will experience salvation out of the mire of sin, as David put it, *"He brought me up also out of an horrible pit, out of the miry clay..."* (Psalm 40:2).

By humbling yourself, you will experience a new victorious life, and then the enemy will lose his hold on you.

Only if you humble yourself will the writing against you be removed: *"Blotting out the handwriting of ordinances that was against us, which was contrary to us, and took it out of the way, nailing it to his cross"* (Colossians 2:14). May God give you grace to truly humble yourself today!   ■

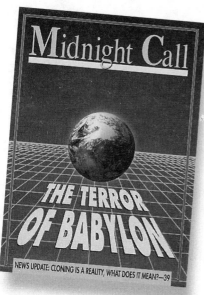